BROOKLYN'S JANE DOE

BROOKLYN'S JANE DOE

The Mishandling of a Sexual Assault Investigation

Sarah A. Mathers

BLOOMSBURY ACADEMIC
NEW YORK • LONDON • OXFORD • NEW DELHI • SYDNEY

BLOOMSBURY ACADEMIC
Bloomsbury Publishing Inc, 1385 Broadway, New York, NY 10018, USA
Bloomsbury Publishing Plc, 50 Bedford Square, London, WC1B 3DP, UK
Bloomsbury Publishing Ireland, 29 Earlsfort Terrace, Dublin 2,
D02 AY28, Ireland
BLOOMSBURY, BLOOMSBURY ACADEMIC and the Diana logo are
trademarks of Bloomsbury Publishing Plc
First published in the United States of America 2025

Cover design by Sally Rinehart
Cover image: © Boogich / iStock Photo / Getty Images

Library of Congress Cataloging-in-Publication Data Available

ISBN: HB: 979-8-8818-0819-8
ePDF: 979-8-8818-4892-7
eBook: 979-8-8818-0820-4

Typeset by Deanta Global Publishing Services, Chennai, India
Printed and bound in the United States of America

For product safety related questions contact productsafety@bloomsbury.com.

To find out more about our authors and books visit www.bloomsbury.com
and sign up for our newsletters.

To Jane Doe, for she never lied

CONTENTS

DISCLAIMER

This book is a faithful reconstruction of my personal experiences as I have recollected them. I have been diligent and deliberate in ensuring that the names and details of events in my book are accurate. Every citation referenced in the book is a matter of public record. Both the claims I assert and the characters portrayed in my book have been described with the highest standard of integrity in mind. Arguments have been built upon both my firsthand experience and publicly available content which undergirds the interpretation of my lived experiences. It never will be and never has been my intention to bring undue hardship or harm to others.

ACKNOWLEDGMENTS

This book would not have been completed without the support and guidance of many remarkable individuals. My deepest thanks to Linda Langton of Langtons International Agency, Rowman & Littlefield, and Bloomsbury Publishing for their unwavering belief that Jane Doe's story needed to be told. I also appreciate the invaluable support from Sonny Marion, Evelin Gutierrez, Anjaly George, Al Bagdonas, Becca Beurer, and Sarah Rinehart. A special thank you to Martin Garbus, Esq., Howard Baum, MD, and my peers and mentors from the Special Victims Division DNA Cold Case Squad, the Brooklyn Special Victims Squad, the Brooklyn DA's Office, the Manhattan DA's Office, and The New York City Office of Chief Medical Examiner for your expertise, guidance, and dedication. I am deeply grateful to Andrea Sorrentino, Keri Thompson, Jimmy Menton, and Michael Osgood. Your persistence, ingenuity, and commitment to solving this case—and all cases—are unparalleled.

Finally, to my family and friends: your unwavering support throughout this journey has meant everything to me.

INTRODUCTION

"I have had the misfortune of being raped twice—once in the park and again in the media," wrote Jane Doe, the victim of an infamous stranger rape in Prospect Park, Brooklyn, in April 1994. Two days after the assault, *New York Daily News* columnist Mike McAlary published a story with the inflammatory headline "Rape hoax the real crime," igniting a media firestorm that questioned the veracity of the victim's account and suggested the crime was fabricated to advance a political agenda. This sensational and irresponsible reporting not only re-victimized Jane Doe but also set in motion a chain of events that would have far-reaching consequences for the victim, the media, and the criminal justice system.

As the case gained national attention, McAlary, rather than retracting his initial claims, doubled down on his stance. He penned two additional columns with equally provocative headlines: "No easy task exposing a lie" and "I'm right, but that's no reason to cheer." These articles further sensationalized the incident, prioritizing the pursuit of a headline over responsible journalism and the well-being of the victim. McAlary's persistence in pushing this narrative, despite mounting evidence to the contrary, demonstrated a troubling disregard for journalistic ethics and the potential harm his words could inflict on a vulnerable individual.

The rush to judgment and the media's eagerness to be first, rather than accurate, inflicted lasting harm on Jane Doe. She faced public ridicule and gaslighting, an experience that not only traumatized her further but also cast a chilling effect on other survivors who feared similar disbelief and public scrutiny. The damage extended beyond Jane Doe, potentially silencing countless other victims who might have otherwise come forward with their own stories of assault. This case became a stark example of how media malpractice can compound the trauma of sexual assault and undermine the pursuit of justice.

The identity of McAlary's source remained a mystery until Jane Doe filed a libel suit against the *Daily News*. Only then, during a court-ordered deposition, was McAlary compelled to reveal his informant. By January 1995, with all leads exhausted and no resolution in sight, the case went cold and remained unsolved for over two decades. This prolonged period of uncertainty and lack of closure undoubtedly took a significant toll on Jane Doe, leaving her to grapple with both the trauma of the assault and the public doubt cast upon her credibility.

It wasn't until October 2017 that a breakthrough finally came. As a founder of the Special Victims DNA Cold Case Squad, I was assigned to reopen the investigation with the support of Commissioner O'Neill. The events that unfolded over the next two months would finally bring a measure of closure to Jane Doe and offer a long-overdue apology for the grave miscarriage of justice she had endured. This development not only provided a chance for justice but also an opportunity for institutional reflection on how cases of sexual assault are handled and reported.

This narrative is an account of one of the most heinous crimes that can be perpetrated against a human being. The people, places, and circumstances described are factual. As a veteran of the New York City Police Department, I've served for 20 years, rising through the ranks from rookie cop to First Grade Detective. New York is a very big city, and we don't have a "Special Victims Unit" like the one that is fictionally portrayed in television shows. There are so many rapists, pederasts, child molesters, grabbers, and abusers who prey on people that the NYPD's Special Victims Division comprises various squads addressing specific crimes across different geographic areas of the city. New York's size and complexity necessitate a comprehensive approach to sex crimes.

When presented with the opportunity to choose a career path as a detective, I had numerous options, including narcotics and the intelligence division. However, driven by a desire to make a meaningful impact, I chose to specialize in an area I believed would help the most people. This decision led me to the challenging yet rewarding field of investigating sex crimes and working to bring justice and closure to survivors. This choice was not made lightly, as it involves confronting some of the darkest aspects of human behavior and supporting survivors through incredibly traumatic experiences.

The decision to specialize in sex crimes investigation comes with unique challenges and responsibilities. It requires not only technical investigative skills but also a high degree of empathy, patience, and emotional resilience. Dealing with victims of sexual assault demands a delicate balance between pursuing justice and supporting the facilitation of a survivor's healing process. It also involves navigating complex societal attitudes toward sexual violence and working to challenge misconceptions and biases that can hinder investigations and re-traumatize victims.

The creation of the Special Victims DNA Cold Case Squad represented a significant step forward in addressing unsolved sexual assault cases. By leveraging advancements in DNA technology and dedicating resources specifically to cold cases, this unit continues to offer hope to survivors who have long-awaited justice. It also sends a powerful message that these crimes are taken seriously, regardless of how much time has passed, and that law enforcement remains committed to solving them.

The Jane Doe case, with its high-profile nature and complex history, presented a unique opportunity to demonstrate the value of this specialized unit. It also offered a chance to right a historical wrong and to showcase how far both law enforcement and society have come in understanding and addressing sexual assault. The reopening of this case was not just about solving a crime but about acknowledging past mistakes, validating a survivor's experience, and working toward a more just and compassionate approach to sexual assault investigations.

As we delve into the details of this case and its resolution, it's important to remember the human element at its core. Behind the headlines and legal proceedings is a survivor who endured not only a brutal assault but also years of public doubt and scrutiny. Her resilience in the face of these challenges is a testament to the strength of the human spirit and a reminder of why the work of the Special Victims DNA Cold Case Squad is so crucial.

Chapter 1

SPECIAL VICTIMS

My first big case was handed to me because there was no one else around to take it. It was a pivotal moment in my career, one that would shape my future in law enforcement and test my mettle as a young officer. It was roughly six months into my new assignment at the Brooklyn Special Victims Squad, a unit known for handling some of the most sensitive and challenging cases in the department. I had been eager to prove myself, but until that day, I had mostly been assisting more experienced detectives.

I walked into work on a day that usually promised a slower pace at the office. Entering the squad room, I was greeted by my Sergeant Tony Samuel, an unruffled seasoned veteran whose expression told me something was brewing. "There's a stranger case in the confines of the 8-4," he said, referring to the precinct that covers the northwestern neighborhoods of Brooklyn, an area I was still getting familiar with. With stranger cases, the investigations are often more complex than those involving known assailants, given the identity of the offender is unknown.

Sergeant Samuel continued, "I haven't heard back from Evelin—looks like it's only you and I today." Evelin was one of our most experienced detectives, and whenever she took time off, her absence was keenly felt.

"The victims at Long Island College Hospital," he added, "and I need someone to head over there." As his words hung in the air, I realized this was my chance to step up, to show that I was ready for more responsibility.

It was common practice within the Special Victims Division for a police officer or "white shield" like myself to have six months of experience under my belt before taking on more significant responsibilities. I needed to prove I could develop competency in handling sensitive cases and become familiar with the procedures that are unique to sex crime investigations. During these initial months, while working closely with Evelin, I'd begun to get a handle on the intricacies of the job, grasp the nuances of working in the Special Victims Division, and begin to hone the skills to handle cases independently.

This included mastering various interview and interrogation techniques, which are vital when dealing with both traumatized victims and potentially manipulative suspects. I was also learning about evidence collection specific to sexual assault cases, the proper handling of rape kits, and the importance of maintaining a sensitive, victim-centered approach throughout my investigation.

I was twenty-seven years old, bright-eyed, and eager to make a difference in the world of law enforcement. My youthful enthusiasm often propelled me forward, sometimes before I had fully thought things through. But in this moment, I felt a surge of confidence, and I responded to my sergeant without skipping a beat, my voice steady despite the butterflies in my stomach, "The only way I'm going to learn is to take this case."

Jumping in at the deep end, Sergeant Samuel and I got into the unmarked police car and drove over to the hospital in silence. The weight of the task ahead settled on my shoulders as I navigated the early morning traffic. During the drive, I found myself rehearsing interview questions in my head, trying to anticipate every possible scenario I might encounter. I tried to remember what I had learned about seeing a crime from different perspectives, including the victim's, the perpetrator's, and my own, in order to piece together an accurate record of the crime that had taken place.

As we parked the car outside the hospital, I took a moment to collect myself. Taking deep breaths to settle my nerves, I grabbed my spiral notebook and stepped out of the vehicle. We walked through the hospital's sliding doors, making our way to the trauma center and a small sequestered room within the ER set up for exactly this purpose.

As Sergeant Samuel and I entered the room, the atmosphere thick, I saw in the victim's eyes a look that spoke volumes about the trauma she had endured. My restless nerves were palpable, filling the air with an almost tangible tension. I realized the enormous responsibility before me, knowing that every word and action from this point on could have a significant impact on the victim and the case.

I tried to sound both firm and empathetic when introducing myself, modulating my tone to strike the right balance. I knew from my training that the first impression could be crucial in establishing trust with a victim. "Good Morning, I'm Police Officer Mathers, but please call me Sarah if you prefer," I said, in a steady voice. I hoped giving her a choice to relate to each other formally or informally would provide a measure of comfort, allowing her to feel more in control of the situation. It was a small gesture, but in moments like these, even the smallest things could make a difference.

"I work at the Brooklyn Special Victims Squad and I've been assigned to your investigation." As the words left my mouth, I couldn't help but wonder if I sounded brash or overconfident. A nagging doubt crept in—*did she care that I wasn't yet a detective? Would she trust me less because of it?* I reminded myself to turn off my inner monologue and to focus on the task at hand.

She looked at both of us, and the first thing she said to me was, "I'll only talk to you. I don't want to talk to a man, I only want to talk to you." My sergeant didn't miss a beat. He quickly acquiesced, stepping out of the small trauma room so that she and I could speak in confidence.

We began with some rapport-building, to help the victim feel more at ease, and we began to discuss the details of her sexual assault. The shaken young woman before me responded to some basic questions, her voice barely above a whisper initially. She began to relay her account of what happened, her voice breaking with emotions and the composure she had been struggling to maintain crumbling, as tears poured down her cheeks, gathering at the corners of her mouth. Her breathing became more labored, and I could see her hands trembling as she described the horrific sexual assault she'd just survived.

"He stole my purse, ripped off my necklace, and raped me," she said, her words coming out in a rush now as if she needed to get them out before her courage failed her. "He made me crawl under a bus and count to sixty. If I didn't crawl under the bus and if I didn't close my eyes, he said he'd kill me." Listening to the brutality of her experience hit me like a physical blow, though I tried to maintain a veneer of impassivity. I told her I'd do my best to find the guy that did this to her, that we'd catch him and bring him to justice, but even as I offered the words, I was uncertain of how reassuring I sounded.

After the interview, walking back to the car, my emotions, which I had kept carefully in check during our conversation, began to surface. My blood was soon boiling as I meditated on the cruelty and senselessness of the crime, thinking to myself, *how could someone do this to another human being*? This poor woman had survived the sexual assault, but in another way, I knew her hell was only just beginning. She would be contending with the long-term repercussions of what had happened to her—the physical healing, the emotional trauma, the potential for PTSD, and the arduous journey through the legal system if we managed to catch the perpetrator. Her strength in the face of such brutality only reinforced my commitment to my chosen career path in the Special Victims Division.

The immediate aftermath of a completed forcible rape presents a critical window for investigation and identification. When the perpetrator's adrenaline is running high, there's an increased likelihood of him making mistakes or leaving evidence that can lead to his capture. Precisely because rapists tend to strike repeatedly, early apprehension can spare countless innocent victims from enduring the same terrifying ordeal. The urgency of this timeframe cannot be overstated, as each day that passes without an arrest increases the risk of additional future assaults.

Several days later, my desk phone rang and it was the store manager from a video game shop where Evelin and I had stopped by a day earlier after chasing down a lead related to the stranger case in the 84th precinct. I had the perpetrator's description the survivor had provided me with the morning I'd interviewed her at Long Island College Hospital though there wasn't enough information she recollected to put together a composite sketch. After stealing her purse, he'd attempted to use her debit card to purchase goods at a game shop in the Fulton Street Mall. We tracked his transactions to the specific storefront and got in touch with the store's manager, gave him a physical description, and asked him to call us right away if the suspect ever came into the store again.

"Officer, the dude is here trying to use the girl's credit card again and you better hurry up." The urgency in the manager's voice prompted our immediate response and thrust us into action, presenting us with a critical opportunity to apprehend the suspect we had been pursuing.

Evelin, who was back on the job, hopped in the driver's seat of our unmarked police minivan; I flipped on the lights and sirens as we sped through traffic. The ride typified the adrenaline-fueled nature of police work, where there are moments of intense action punctuated by long periods of tedious detective work. Evelin's quick thinking and extreme driving skills would prove crucial in what was about to unfold.

We flew down Washington Avenue to Atlantic Avenue and from Atlantic onto Fulton, veering into the bus lane. All the while the store manager stayed on the phone, his gaze discreetly following the guy for the time he remained in the store. This real-time coordination exemplified the collaborative effort often required in successful police operations.

Arriving into the local area, the store manager confirmed the direction the perp had set out on, on foot, after having left the store. Evelin tactically maneuvered our vehicle onto a curb, getting us within a safe distance to intercept our target. We jumped out of the car and we handcuffed him just as a crowd began to gather. With the perpetrator successfully apprehended, we called for a transport vehicle. Our job was done and we headed back to the squad.

Though I was convinced we had the right perpetrator, we were unable to charge him with first-degree rape because he had a solid alibi placing him at the single-room occupancy (SRO) he was residing in during the time of the alleged rape. Covering his bases, he had someone at the SRO sign him in, though unbeknownst to staff, he was not on the premises. Upon questioning him, he claimed that he'd picked up the purse after finding it discarded on the road and made no allusions to the sexual assault. While I was intent on holding him to a lesser charge, ultimately I had to let him go until there was more convincing evidence. I had a hunch that this would not be his first and only criminal offense, and while I was eager to solve my first major case, I learned patience was a virtue.

Time passed—months and then years. While a male DNA profile had been successfully extracted from a semen stain on the survivor's jeans, early on in the investigation, there was no matching DNA sample for the offender found in CODIS, the national DNA database. I had his name and in the time after the investigation closed, I would run a cross-check on the name whenever this case sprang to mind. But there was nothing concrete linking the sexual assault to the suspect we'd arrested until a day in 2013 when I was at my desk looking through my case log in ECMS, the enterprise case management system where all cases are electronically archived, and I saw a DNA hit to the survivor's name, indicating there was a DNA profile in CODIS that matched to the collected semen sample from my case years earlier. This news prompted such a visceral reaction in me that I let out a scream.

Finally, we had our guy. In 2012, the DNA collection law changed in New York to include penal law misdemeanors, not just felony-level or violent crimes. So, any person convicted of a misdemeanor would have to submit a DNA sample which would then be stored in the New York State DNA Databank. My theory that this man who had committed rape would continue to commit other crimes had panned out to be true.

It was time to find out where he was, and I tracked him down at an inpatient halfway house for residents who were in drug rehab. Because it was a court-mandated program, I was not able to make an immediate arrest, but there was now enough to prosecute.

The wheels of the justice system are notorious for moving with glacial slowness, and when it came time to prepare for the trial, the survivor had moved on with her life. She didn't want to revisit the horror she had suffered; in her mind, she had closed that door behind her forever. This passage of time between the crime and potential trial is a common challenge in the criminal justice system, often placing additional burdens on victims who may have worked hard to move past their traumatic experiences.

The prosecutor took the survivor's wishes into consideration and a plea deal was made. She did not need to testify in court to relive her worst day. While plea deals can be controversial, because negotiations are resolved behind closed doors and without the benefit of a full trial, in cases such as this one a plea deal can serve to protect a victim from further trauma while still ensuring some measure of justice is served. The decision to offer a plea deal often involves considering various factors, including the strength of the evidence, the victim's wishes, and the resources of the justice system.

This investigation meant a lot to me as a young police officer because it reinforced in my mind the importance of justice playing its full hand, both deterring others and reassuring victims that the offense that disrupted their lives won't happen again. That became a central theme of my police career, wanting to make our streets safer for all, women in particular. You never forget your first major investigation, and though it took years to come to fruition, the experience I garnered at the Brooklyn Special Victims Squad solidified my desire to solve cases related to sex crimes. When I got to Special Victims in 2008, I found I had a talent for solving needle-in-a-haystack cases, as so many of them are. Following are the top five sexual assault cases that stretched me in ways that undoubtedly made me a stronger investigator and fueled my desire to establish a DNA Cold Case Squad for sexual assaults.

In March of 2010, Evelin and I were investigating a vicious stranger rape case where the perpetrator had raped, pistol-whipped, and shot at a fifty-six-year-old woman, who narrowly survived the vicious attack. The victim had left her apartment in the Clinton Hill neighborhood of Brooklyn after midnight to stop in at her local bodega for a cigarette run. On the short walk home, she is approached by a young man who, asking for a smoke, casually places his arm around her shoulder, bringing her into close contact.

According to the victim's account, she saw the silhouette of a firearm clutched by his available hand and pointed directly at her from beneath his sweatshirt. The sight petrifies the woman, whom he forces into submission, saying, "You're gonna walk with me, you're effing coming with me," taking her to the back entrance of a nearby park in Clinton Hill, just adjacent to an elementary school.

He leads her down a set of stairs to the basement room landing outside a maintenance closet where he proceeds to pistol whip her across the forehead and face leaving a giant laceration, for which she'd receive seventy-six stitches. He proceeds to brutally rape her and terrifies her further by penetrating her with the barrel of the gun. Following the sexual assault, as she attempts to fight him off, he takes a shot at her, the bullet missing her by inches before he flees the crime scene, leaving her abandoned and bleeding with her pants around her ankles. A neighbor hears a gunshot followed by screams for help and places an anonymous 911 call, directing uniformed officers to the area where she is found and taken immediately to a hospital.

Evelin and I arrive at the hospital and as I'm interviewing the victim, I cannot help but observe that the physical injuries she has sustained are so extensive that I believe she was lucky to be found alive. It was mid-afternoon by the time Evelin and I left the hospital and drove around Clinton Hill. While there was no community-wide network of CCTV cameras, many individual business owners had exterior security cameras installed, and there was likely footage of our perpetrator which could provide us with valuable leads. As we continued to scout the neighborhood, we encountered a mentally ill woman, who appeared homeless and was urinating in the street. A week later, the day before St. Patrick's Day, this vulnerable woman is targeted as the young perpetrator's next victim. His MO is consistent, in how he approaches and subdues her, with the arm around the shoulder, bringing her into close contact and revealing he's armed, raping her in a grassy alleyway between two buildings. After the assault, he also commits theft when he makes off with her cell phone, an act that would ultimately lead to his capture.

Both victims are able to provide a description and key information unique to the suspect. He looked to be in his mid-twenties, wearing a black Yankees hat. He chain-smoked Newport cigarettes and used more than one condom while violating his victims. We got a sketch out and then contacted TARU, the Technical Assistance Response Unit, a specialized unit that provides technological expertise, through which we were able to obtain a subpoena for the mobile phone carrier and get authorized for a trap and trace warrant for the victim's phone. The warrant enables our team at TARU to track the location of the cell phone by sending a signal to it and tracing the electronic data.

It was while we were on a seven-day canvas in the field with the first victim that we received a ping, a notification from the victim's phone. Her stolen cell phone was clearly still in use and within minutes we were able to triangulate the location, with a high degree of accuracy, to a house party in Brooklyn. We quickly got a team set up to apprehend the suspect. It was Evelin, who had the house party shut down, but not before she stopped five of the partygoers who fit the description. They cooperated voluntarily and were brought into the precinct to be interviewed one at a time. Upon being patted down, one of the five suspects was discovered with Newports and a bunch of condoms in his pockets. This young man consented to DNA collection, a buccal swab of the cells lining the inside of his cheeks, perhaps believing he'd left no DNA at the crime scene or in the victims' bodies. Several days later, we obtained a search warrant for his apartment, and the firearm that he used to threaten both rape victims was recovered. As a defendant, the evidence against him was overwhelming. He ended up accepting a plea deal and was incarcerated thereafter.

In another case, I was assigned to a task force to take down a serial rapist. A homicide of a sex worker in the Red Hook area of the 76th precinct, Brooklyn, had gone unsolved until a city-wide pattern was established, across multiple boroughs, linking five rape cases involving sex workers through case-to-case DNA matches. We had a description of the perpetrator, as a thin, Black male in his forties who walked with a characteristic swagger. After a few months of following up on leads, following a rape in the Bronx, a brilliant colleague of mine, Jimmy Menton, went to track where the sex workers were known to be active. He befriended a number of them and confirmed that there was a fellow by the name of Mark who fit the description to a tee. With this fresh lead, I began to mine the data, all the while trying to get inside the head of the perpetrator. If I were Mark, what places would I be frequenting?

Many of the victims were sex workers who had been approached in public parks, so I began to cross-check the names of those who'd been issued park summonses for minor infractions like loitering. I also combed through police reports, crossing-checking the name "Mark" or "Marc" with those who had prior arrest histories in the specific neighborhoods where the rapes had occurred.

One of the rape victims confirmed that she'd been raped in the stairwell inside a building in which her attacker had claimed to know a relative. This narrowed our search, and we soon had a last name and a DMV photo of our prime suspect, a man named Mark White. Tracking him down at his place of employment, where he worked as a security guard at a coop based in the Bronx. We followed him for a seventy-two-hour period, and we were eventually able to retrieve his DNA, from an abandonment sample, and put him away.

In another case, my partner Jonathan and I were doing an early morning seven-day canvass, investigating another stranger's sex assault in which the victim had described her attacker as a lanky, light-colored, man who had fled the crime scene on a yellow bicycle.

Time was of the essence, and we had little more than a description to get our investigation underway. Then, while canvassing in the Fort Greene area of Brooklyn, a radio dispatch came in from an anonymous unverified complainant who placed a 911 call to report a suspicious male on a yellow bike who was peering through the window of a property at a given location. Sometimes solving an investigation hinges on the merit of one detail that creates the necessary momentum.

We rushed to the address, unsure of what we were about to face. When we first encountered him, we noticed something in his pockets. We stopped him at gunpoint, but soon holstered our weapons, and began speaking. Without probable cause for an arrest, there was no way to bring him back to the precinct unless he wanted to come back with us voluntarily. With his patent refusal, we had no choice but to let him go as making an arrest based on an anonymous 911 call would have been a violation of his constitutional right against unreasonable search and seizure.

I documented his name and with a high degree of confidence he was culpable for the sexual assaults my partner and I were investigating, we headed back to the precinct to do a workup on him. While still learning the ropes, it was in this case that I was again reminded of the value of exercising restraint and not forcing the natural course of justice. When he committed another attempted rape, the survivor was able to identify him, which led to his arrest for multiple cases of assault.

I was gaining a reputation among my colleagues for my keen ability to mine the data and the minute details of an investigative case. My peers would seek out my help, often when they were stumped and unable to find a break in their case. A colleague was struggling to identify a perpetrator of a stranger sexual assault in Brooklyn who notably had a tattoo on his face. While the rapist eluded capture for the attack in Brooklyn, the very next day he was in Manhattan committing another sexual assault and was immediately apprehended.

While cross-borough communication between detectives can take some time, his arrest photo, taken when he was processed at Manhattan Central Booking, had already been uploaded to the NYPD photo database. While sifting through thousands of arrest photos, I could filter the search results using keywords. Limiting my search to those with facial tattoos, we were able to identify the suspect right away and could charge him with assaults.

From 2011 to 2013, a serial rapist pretending to be a livery driver had gone under the radar for nearly two years in the Williamsburg and Bushwick neighborhoods, leaving a trail of victims behind. In 2013, I assisted my colleague in which a victim had been grabbed off the street and the perpetrator attempted to rape her in the back seat of his large black GMC Yukon.

He had an MO in which he would pick up his victims, who were hailing cabs, and while en route to their destination, he would then pull over to the side of the road and jump into the back seat of the car. Some incidents resulted in complaints of harassment, so not every encounter escalated to rape. With some women, he would try to seduce them, touching them inappropriately and dancing suggestively, going as far as to give those he was interested in a fake name and phone number.

Acquiring the phone number from a victim who had managed to flee the vehicle, I ran it through an NYPD database which matched zero records. Then I ran multiple searches using just a partial phone number, the last six digits, and the last three digits and found a slew of complaint reports on file. One of these reports detailed a harassment complaint in which a livery cab driver jumped into the back seat with the complainant and began dancing. That report listed a license plate number from which I was able to pull his real name, his photo, and his address on record. We showed up at his place in Brooklyn and apprehended him. When the District Attorney asked me how I tracked down a culprit who was operating under a fake name and address, I shared my hunch that most people create aliases and counterfeit numbers that are never too far from the actual truth. In this case, the perpetrator, whose name was David, was going by the name Danny, which was his brother's name, and most of the digits in the so-called fake phone number were a slight variation of his actual phone number.

In 2011, I pitched the idea of establishing a DNA Cold Case Squad for sexual assaults to a group of Special Victims Division supervisors. This initiative was born out of a recognition that advances in DNA technology could potentially solve cases that had long gone cold, bringing justice to victims who had been waiting for years. Despite the potential of this initiative, my proposal was tabled for reasons that weren't entirely transparent to me. Perhaps it was due to budget constraints, or maybe the department wasn't ready for such a specialized unit. Whatever the cause, my idea was put on hold, seemingly destined to gather dust in the archives of unrealized potential. However, fate had a way of intervening in unexpected ways.

With a background in investigating hate crimes, NYPD Detective Bureau Deputy Police Chief Michael J. Osgood was an agent for positive change for many years in the NYPD Special Victims Division, right up until the point he was ousted from the department in 2018. By that time, he was the Commanding Officer of the Special Victims Division. His departure followed a heated political imbroglio that derailed the unit, leaving it in shambles when left without the clear leadership that someone of Chief Osgood's stature could provide.

A lot of the higher-ups, those who made up the NYPD brass, didn't always agree with the way Osgood chose to do things, as their mentalities and practices could seem both fixed and antiquated by Osgood's standards. Being an intelligent force of nature, savant-like in his ability to think outside of the box, he, inevitably, drew adoration and criticism alike. Despite some controversies, he was held in high esteem and was overwhelmingly respected by community advocates and heralded by women's groups as heroic for his unwavering dedication to being pro-victim in his investigative work.

With Chief Osgood at the helm, operations within the Special Victims Division were true-blue in its reputation of being a victim-centered model. In Osgood's eyes, every victim was on an equal footing. It didn't matter about your background, be it lack of privilege afforded to others, or your sexual orientation, every victim deserved to have an advocate and to be treated with dignity and respect.

In 2013, the Broadway play *Lucky Guy*, written by celebrated American screenwriter and playwright Nora Ephron, premiered at the Broadhurst Theatre. It was based on the life of *New York Daily News* investigative journalist and tabloid columnist Mike McAlary, who passed away after a controversial career in 1998. With actor Tom Hanks playing the leading role of the reporter, the play's script includes mention of a news story McAlary ran with and printed on April 28th of 1994 titled, "Rape hoax the real crime."

On a June afternoon, upon hearing a radio ad for Ephron's play while driving into work, Chief Mike Osgood felt compelled to pull the case folder detailing this sexual assault in Brooklyn's Prospect Park; nineteen years old, it had never been solved. Upon reviewing its contents, he had the renewed conviction that the case could have been solved years earlier, possibly even before the perpetrator struck again if only it had been afforded a more comprehensive analysis of the data available. What a difference this would have made to the victim, and to the subsequent rape victims, who might have never endured what befell them if Jane Doe's rapist had been caught sooner.

Osgood wasted no time in emailing then Chief of Detectives Phil Pulaski in June of 2013, about his renewed interest in relaunching the investigation and looking into the cold case, and while this may have moved the needle in the right direction, it didn't ultimately convince the NYPD brass, whose corroboration would be needed. Plans to reopen the case were once again kiboshed.

Arguably, one valid good reason *not* to dredge up details of a cold case from 1994 could be to keep untarnished the reputations of those who were still serving as of 2013—long-time veterans of the police force, who may have played a role, either large or small, when details of the case first splashed across New York City newspapers.

Two years later, in 2015, the stars aligned to bring the prospect of establishing a DNA Cold Case Squad for sexual assaults back into the realm of possibilities. This renewed interest may have been indicative of a shift in departmental priorities and significant DNA advances in the time since these cases initially went unsolved, boosting the likelihood of solving them. These technological improvements have made it a far more likely occurrence to identify perpetrators and link them to their crimes, adding enormously to the effectiveness of cold case operations. The evolution of DNA analysis techniques has been nothing short of revolutionary in the field of forensic science. Methods that were once nonexistent or in their nascency when many of these cases first occurred are now capable of extracting DNA profiles from even the smallest or most degraded samples.

My plan for reopening these cold cases, where permission was granted to investigate, was multifaceted and driven by a deep sense of justice and compassion. My primary goal was to bring long-delayed or previously denied justice to victims who continued to suffer for never having received restitution or compensation for their pain, left to bear both the emotional and financial burdens of their trauma alone. By solving these cases, I hoped to lift the weight of misplaced societal blame that many victims had internalized over the years. For those who had been living with unresolved trauma, I wanted my efforts to help shift the perception of guilt onto their perpetrators, where it rightfully belonged.

Oftentimes, the success of these cold cases depended heavily on the survivor's willingness to reignite the formal investigation process. This decision is not made lightly, as it meant re-living the horror of their past experience—a memory that the passage of time may have helped a survivor to cope with or at least compartmentalize. The prospect of reopening old wounds and confronting long-buried traumas could be daunting for many survivors. It required immense courage and strength to step forward and engage with the legal system once again, especially when the outcome remained uncertain. As an investigator, I had to approach these situations with the utmost sensitivity and respect.

Unlike homicide cases where the victim is tragically killed, survivors of sexual assault often live on, carrying the weight of their experiences with them. This means they have to deal with the painful long-term ramifications of the assault, such as post-traumatic stress disorder, anxiety, depression, and a host of other challenges following such violent encounters. The impact of sexual assault can permeate every aspect of a survivor's life, affecting their relationships, career, and overall well-being. When a case goes unsolved, such stress can be particularly acute and long-lasting.

I like to think that every crime solved not only puts the perpetrator behind bars, where they can no longer harm innocent people, but it also has a broader deterrent effect that makes potential criminals think twice before committing similar offenses. By demonstrating that justice can still be served, even years later, we send a powerful message to would-be offenders that their actions have consequences, no matter how much time has passed.

Chapter 2

"WE DON'T BELIEVE HER"

In the time after the DNA Cold Case Squad got underway, it was thanks to the advocacy of my former sergeant Keri Thompson that I was well positioned and in line to accept Jane Doe's case as lead detective when the case reopened. Thompson convinced Chief Osgood, who sat down with Chief of Detectives Robert Boyce and Police Commissioner James O'Neill. With support from the brass, who both greenlighted the idea, Thompson and Osgood assigned Brooklyn's Jane Doe case to me in October 2017.

Being less than rigorous with journalistic best practices such as fact-checking, McAlary, who passed away at the young age of forty-one from colon cancer, was known to spend time at favorite New York watering holes like Elaine's during the mid-1990s. His frequent companions included then-New York City Police Commissioner William Bratton and others who made up the NYPD's elite. These social gatherings provided an informal setting where information and gossip flowed freely, blurring the lines between professional relationships and personal rapport.

McAlary's presence in these circles granted him unprecedented access to high-ranking officials and insider information, a position many journalists would envy. However, this proximity to power and privileged information came with its own set of risks and ethical challenges. The casual nature of these interactions could lead to a false sense of reliability in the information shared, potentially compromising the objectivity and thoroughness required in responsible journalism. Comments shared and intended to be strictly off-the-record might be mistaken for factual information that could potentially lead to the publication of unverified rumors, running the risk of jeopardizing ongoing investigations and the privacy of victims.

It's not hard to extrapolate how spending any amount of time in the company of this cadre of men could result in an overreliance on them as sources of news for any upcoming article McAlary was working on. The allure of exclusive information and the thrill of being an insider could be intoxicating, potentially clouding a journalist's commitment to thoroughly vetting the content of the information he's received. As a more seasoned veteran of the newsroom, perhaps McAlary found taking some chances by relying on juicy scoops from insiders was preferable to pounding the pavement, wearing down the leather soles of one's shoes, to chase leads for the next day's news cycle.

However, for stories reporting on crimes, in which getting the facts straight was an essential part of the journalist's obligation to uphold the truth, this was inherently dysfunctional as negligence resulting from an overreliance on this approach was a foregone conclusion. Accepting information at face value and forgoing comprehensive, ground-level fact-checking could likely lead to the publication of inaccurately reported or biased stories. A scoop could be less than credible, or dubious enough to be unfit to print, and the motivations behind sharing certain information might not have always aligned with the public interest or journalistic integrity. It was only a matter of time before such a lapse in good judgment, on McAlary's part, would inevitably occur. The pressure to maintain his status as a top columnist, combined with the competitive nature of New York's media landscape, could easily lead to cutting corners in the pursuit of a headline-grabbing story.

In a rush to print, this seems to be exactly what happened the day Mike McAlary's first column, which hit the newsstands on April 28, 1994, ran under the headline: "Rape hoax the real crime." This provocative headline, based on information gleaned from his police sources, would prove to be a critical misstep in McAlary's career. The decision to run with such a sensational claim without thorough verification not only violated journalistic ethics but also had profound consequences for the victim of the alleged crime.

Leaked misinformation was printed as news, and there was heavy speculation in the days afterward that McAlary's source was either Deputy Commissioner of Public Information, John Miller, or former Chief of Department, John Timoney. The controversy surrounding the source of McAlary's information highlighted the complex and often murky relationship between law enforcement officials and the media, raising questions about the ethical responsibilities of journalists when writing about cases that are actively being investigated.

Nora Ephron's play made an oblique reference to Timoney, casting some shade on his sterling reputation, suggesting that even respected figures in law enforcement could be implicated in the mishandling of sensitive information. Miller only ever admitted to "mischaracterizing our conversation," referring to words exchanged with the *New York Daily News* reporter. This carefully worded admission, while acknowledging some level of miscommunication, fell short of taking full responsibility for the misinformation that was leaked.[1] As Miller's working title of Deputy Commissioner of Public Information suggests, his professional duties encompassed the dissemination of information cleared by the NYPD to be shared publicly. However, in speaking with McAlary, Miller may never have considered that a casual conversation with Mike would be taken word-for-word as an on-the-record account. He may have taken it for granted in assuming that McAlary knew whatever words were exchanged between the two men was off-the-record and not intended to be received as though Miller were speaking in an official capacity.

McAlary never met with the victim Jane Doe and never got her account firsthand, a glaring omission in his reporting that undermined the credibility of his claims. His written assertion that she was spinning yarn to fulfill a personal political agenda[2] reads with a bombastic air of accusation. Relying heavily on unnamed sources without seeking direct input from the victim raised ethical questions about journalistic practices in a story involving sexual assault. In addition, by relying solely on secondary sources, McAlary deprived himself and his readers of a context and perspective that perhaps would have significantly altered or tempered what he wrote. If McAlary had cared to make a stronger attempt to corroborate the truth of Jane Doe's claims, he would likely have done the legwork to reach out to more sources. Given their input, he would have had the chance to balance or examine more thoughtfully claims that appeared to contradict each other.

McAlary also admitted to never visiting Prospect Park, the scene of the crime, in the days while he was reporting on this story. This lack of on-the-ground investigation further highlighted the lack of any substantive reporting on the case and suggests that McAlary was only intending to write about the case superficially—as he could not have anticipated the media firestorm that would erupt following the first column. Despite these significant gaps in his research and firsthand knowledge, he would go on to write two additional columns, defending his stance, in light of the heavy public scrutiny after the *New York Post*, and other media outlets, validated the accuracy of Jane Doe's allegations about what happened to her on April 26th, based on the findings from the Medical Examiner's Office.[3] McAlary's persistence in maintaining his position, even as contradictory evidence emerged, demonstrated a troubling reluctance to acknowledge errors in the face of new information. His unwillingness to reconsider his position in light of new findings was a poor decision that was a reflection of his professional hubris.

As the media hype around the story grew, McAlary's other two headlines, "No easy task exposing a lie," and "I'm right, but that's no reason to cheer," show the stubbornness of a man doubling down, refusing to recognize the truth and in a defensive posture with the emphatic need to defend himself in print. These follow-up pieces not only compounded the harm done to Jane Doe but also perpetuated a false narrative. As other media outlets presented evidence supporting Jane Doe's account, McAlary remained entrenched in his original position, failing to prioritize truth over his reputation, endangering both in the process.

In a personal statement Jane Doe released to the Gay and Lesbian Anti-Violence Project,[4] she lamented, "I must say I have no idea why some police 'investigators' chose to release inaccurate, misleading, and ultimately exploitative information about my experience. If their desire was to scare women away from reporting rape, they succeeded." This poignant statement highlighted the broader implications of the mishandling of her case, suggesting that irresponsible reporting and police leaks could have a chilling effect on other victims coming forward. Jane Doe continued, "I have had the misfortune of being raped twice—once in the park and again in the media.[5] I hope Mike McAlary and all the vultures making their living off my pain sleep better than I will tonight." This stark comparison between the physical assault and the media's treatment of her story underscored the profound detrimental impact that irresponsible journalism can have on victims of crime. By equating McAlary's columns to a second rape, Jane Doe makes no bones about its re-traumatizing effect. Arguably, her condemnation could also extend to the far-reaching consequences of the NYPD mishandling her sexual assault case, which led to the media debacle that followed.

In McAlary's first column, "Rape Hoax the real crime," he describes Jane Doe as someone with an active imagination who fed skeptical cops an outrageous story that he called pure fiction. His portrayal of Jane Doe was both dismissive and accusatory, suggesting that she had fabricated a serious crime for personal gain. While questioning Jane Doe's status as a rape survivor, characterizing the victim of a sexual assault with anything less than the most empathetic language reads as incredibly tone-deaf to the suffering experienced by rape victims. His language is both heavy-handed and inflammatory.

McAlary's column implied that Jane Doe's actions were not just deceitful but also socially irresponsible, claiming that she cried wolf, scaring a whole city in the process for fear that Prospect Park in Brooklyn had once again become a hotbed for criminal activity. This characterization painted Jane Doe as a manipulative individual, a conniving perpetrator of the public trust, who disregarded the potential consequences of her alleged false report on community safety and resources.

Contrary to McAlary's depiction, Jane Doe's background suggests a very different person. Raised in the Midwest, she was a Yale University graduate and a recent transplant to the Brooklyn area, sharing a home with several roommates. Like many recent graduates who flock to New York City to begin their work lives as young professionals, she was pursuing an acting career while working a day job as a receptionist. McAlary largely ignored this context and instead portrayed Jane Doe as someone who fabricated a serious crime for attention or political purposes. Having maligned her in his columns, portraying her as deviant, rather than as a young woman focused on building a career and life for herself in a new city, he skewed the public perception of Jane Doe and her credibility.

McAlary carried his argument further by claiming that Jane Doe had concocted the whole story in service of an appearance at a rally that was scheduled for the weekend following the Tuesday afternoon rape. This assertion suggested a level of calculated manipulation that seemed at odds with the trauma typically experienced by sexual assault survivors. McAlary implies that Jane Doe was willing to *act as if* she'd been raped, subjecting herself to invasive medical examinations, police questioning, and public scrutiny, merely to promote a political cause.

The survivor, likely shaken to her core from what transpired, did not speak in person at the rally in Park Slope sponsored by the Gay and Lesbian Anti-Violence Project, though she'd prepared a statement that was read aloud on her behalf by friends and colleagues. This decision to have others speak for her, rather than appearing personally, could be seen as consistent with the behavior of someone dealing with the aftermath of a traumatic experience, rather than someone seeking publicity. The choice to remain out of the public eye is consistent with the behavior of someone dealing with the aftermath of a traumatic experience. The fact that she had prepared a statement at all, despite the recent trauma and public skepticism, spoke to her courage even in the face of personal adversity. McAlary's portrayal of Jane Doe as an attention-seeker who is hungry for publicity falls flat.

Subsequently, Matt Foreman, the Executive Director of the Gay and Lesbian Anti-Violence Project, defended Jane Doe's reputation from such public flogging by a member of the press. He suggested that McAlary's brash assumptions may have been spurred on by his homophobia, introducing the possibility that prejudice was driving McAlary's narrative. This accusation highlighted the intersectionality of the issues at play—not just sexual assault but also discrimination against the LGBTQIA+ community. Foreman's intervention brought attention to the bias that can influence how journalists like McAlary cover stories of those belonging to marginalized communities.

In contrast to McAlary's approach, Foreman had words of praise for New York City's Police Commissioner William J. Bratton's proactive gesture to issue an apology on April 29, 1994, three days after the rape and a day after McAlary's first column ran. While the apology was largely about optics, as a way to staunch a gaffe that had the potential to embarrass the police department, nevertheless, Foreman said, "I respect Commissioner Bratton for his comments. His response stands far ahead of what any police commissioner has done or would have done under similar circumstances."[6] Foreman's commendation of Bratton's response suggests that Bratton's response was both progressive and compassionate for the time. By publicly addressing possible errors in the initial handling of Jane Doe's case, Bratton demonstrated a level of accountability and gutsiness uncommon for police leadership at the time. His foresight in being proactive helped to mitigate potential damage to the department's reputation.

The day after McAlary's first column riled readers, Commissioner Bratton offered these words, publicly saying, "Investigations take time to go where the truth will take you. Apparently, in this incident, there were some significant leaps made to arrive at certain conclusions that are not being borne out."[7] His willingness to extend an olive branch of diplomacy was to be commended, as it represented a rare instance of a high-ranking official admitting to potential missteps in an ongoing investigation. Bratton's statement also acknowledged the complexity of sexual assault investigations and signaled to the public and to survivors that the police department was committed to thorough and fair investigations. By reassuring the public that the NYPD was committed to uncovering the truth, he indirectly critiqued the rush to judgment evident in McAlary's reporting. Furthermore, Bratton's words offered a measure of support to Jane Doe, implicitly validating her experience and the importance of taking all sexual assault allegations seriously.

Bratton's measured response was a stark contrast to McAlary's sensationalized reporting, a powerful illustration of the different approaches to handling sensitive information. While McAlary's columns prioritized shock value and speculation, at the expense of the victim's well-being and the integrity of the investigation, Bratton's statement emphasized forbearance and a commitment to uncovering the truth. Both are juxtaposing examples of how communication plays a key role in shaping public perception.

Victims' rights advocate Susan Rios of the Coalition Against Sexual Assault also came to Jane Doe's defense in critiquing McAlary's reporting and its potential impact on sexual assault survivors. Her statement reflected the deep concern and frustration felt by many advocates in the field of sexual violence prevention and victim support. "We reacted to this with sadness, disappointment, and outrage," Rios said, encapsulating the complex emotions stirred by McAlary's columns. Her words highlighted the profound effect that such public skepticism, resulting from the ripple effect of irresponsible journalism, can have on survivors of sexual assault and the broader community of advocates who work tirelessly to combat sexual violence.

Rios went on to articulate the dangerous implications of McAlary's approach, stating, "The message here to rape victims is, 'Keep it to yourself.'"[8] This succinct observation cuts to the heart of the issue, emphasizing how media narratives that question or dismiss survivors' accounts can contribute to a culture of silence and shame surrounding sexual assault. Such a message, Rios implied, could deter other victims from coming forward, seeking help, or reporting their assaults to authorities. This potential chilling effect is a significant concern for advocates who work indefatigably to create an environment where survivors feel supported and believed.

Rios's statement served as a pointed critique of McAlary's reporting and underscored the power that media coverage has to either empower or discourage survivors when such a force plays a large role in shaping societal attitudes around sexual assault. A real-world consequence of castigating victims in media narratives is the discouraging effect on those survivors willing to report, which may ultimately strangle the pursuit of justice for many sexual assault survivors. Many advocates face ongoing challenges in combating deeply ingrained societal attitudes about sexual assault. Rape victims themselves, in their lives before and after their sexual assault, have internalized these attitudes, casting a long pall over their future choices.

McAlary's lead paragraph, in this first column, opens in Boston, 1989, with the story of Charles "Chuck" Stuart,[9] who killed his wife for the insurance money but threw investigators off the scent of the trail by claiming a black man had fired the fatal bullet. Before his plum assignment as a New York columnist, McAlary had first launched his journalism career as a reporter in Boston, so he may have been well-versed in the lurid details of this Boston-based story.

McAlary wrote, "Stuart's fiction became a racial parable for our times. In Brooklyn, you fear today, someone has tried to ruin part of this city with the same lie," before delving into the details of the crime in Prospect Park. He later writes, "A false report of rape by a woman looking for publicity is a crime against all women. It diminishes all rape victims." While this assertion in and of itself can be true, the errant accusation against Jane Doe, who was not looking for publicity and who was truthful about what happened to her, is equally diminishing to rape victims. McAlary committed a great disservice in assuming Jane Doe's guilt or dishonesty without sufficient evidence. McAlary committed the very act he condemns by diminishing the experience of a rape victim, perpetuating the cycle of undermining the credibility of sexual assault survivors.

In his subsequent column which ran under the headline, "No easy task exposing a lie," McAlary delves deeper into the complexities of proving false allegations in rape cases. He draws a parallel between the infamous Tawana Brawley case and Jane's investigation in Brooklyn, highlighting the challenges faced by law enforcement in such situations. McAlary writes, "In the beginning, there was Tawana Brawley and the rape that never happened. The question, then and now, is how do you prove a lie? How can the cops in Brooklyn, for example, prove that this week's hoaxer wasn't raped the other night in Prospect Park?"

This comparison serves to frame the current case within a broader context of high-profile false rape allegations, implicitly suggesting a pattern of deception. By drawing this parallel, McAlary risks conflating two separate cases with different circumstances, potentially prejudicing readers against Jane Doe before all the facts are known. McAlary emphasizes the dilemma faced by the police: "They know she lied, but they're letting her fade away, worried that genuine victims might not come forward." McAlary then draws a contrast with the Brawley case, noting, "Brawley, of course, did not fade away. Without a shred of evidence, her lawyer accused innocent people," highlighting the potential consequences of false allegations when they gain significant public attention and legal momentum. His comparison oversimplifies the complexities of both cases.

Tawana Brawley[10] was a fifteen-year-old African American cheerleader who became the center of a national controversy in 1987 and 1988. Her case dominated front-page news before and after investigators proved she had fabricated her rape claim. Brawley's allegation that she was assaulted by a group of white men in the grassy knoll behind her family's apartment complex north of New York City captivated public attention and ignited heated debates about race, gender, and justice in

America. The case became a flashpoint for discussions about racial tensions and the treatment of sexual assault victims in the media and legal system.

The gravity of Brawley's accusations was amplified when she claimed in a televised interview that one of her attackers was a police officer. This explosive allegation instigated a national media blitz, drawing intense scrutiny from all corners of society. The case attracted the involvement of well-known New York legal minds, including Alton H. Maddox Jr., C. Vernon Mason, and the Reverend Al Sharpton Jr., who stepped in to advise Brawley. Their involvement elevated the case from a local crime story to a national debate on racial injustice and police misconduct, further complicating an already sensitive situation.

With a racial epithet scrawled across Tawana Brawley's chest in large ashen letters, the case took on even more sinister overtones when Harry Crist Jr., a Caucasian police officer who died from a self-inflicted gunshot wound to the head, in the days immediately following the supposed November 1987 assault, added fuel to a raging fire of speculation. This tragic turn of events further intensified the racial tensions surrounding the case, adding to an already volatile situation.

In response to these developments, Rev. Sharpton, known for his provocative and often polarizing statements, declared in his signature showboating style, "New York State is now the capital of racial violence." This proclamation was not merely a comment on the Brawley case but a broader indictment of racial relations in New York and, by extension, the United States. Sharpton's words heaped scores of additional notoriety onto an already inflammatory story, further polarizing people along lines of gender, race, and the specter of police misconduct. The case became a lightning rod for discussions about systemic racism, the credibility afforded to victims of different races, and the role of media in shaping public perception of high-profile criminal cases.

By October of 1988, a grand jury had thoroughly investigated the Tawana Brawley case and reached a conclusion that would have far-reaching consequences. The jury discredited Brawley's rape allegations as pure fabrication, a finding that would become the enduring legacy of the case. This outcome cast a long shadow on the credibility of genuine rape victims everywhere, creating a climate of skepticism that would prove challenging to overcome. The fact that Brawley, a woman of color, was found to have lied about her assault had damaging repercussions for other women of color who came forward with allegations of sexual violence.

The fallout from the Brawley case created an environment where victims like Brooklyn's Jane Doe found themselves increasingly vulnerable to being pegged as so-called copycats or attention-seekers. The assumption that a victim is no victim at all, but rather a liar or fantasist, became the unfortunate legacy of the Tawana Brawley hoax,[11] posing a significant challenge to the credibility of all sexual assault survivors, but especially women of color, who often faced additional barriers and stereotypes when reporting crimes.

For the long-suffering Jane Doe, who is now in her mid-fifties and working in the health and wellness field, new developments in forensic DNA analysis twenty-three years after the assault would prove that she was telling the truth all along. The two-decade-long wait for justice highlights the profound impact that advances in forensic science can have on cold cases and the lives of those involved. For Jane Doe, the reopening of her case represented a pivotal moment in her quest for vindication, after being marked for many years by the experience of public scrutiny. The prevalence of DNA evidence to solve cases continues to prompt debate about the role of evolving technology in the legal system. With ongoing capital investment in forensic science, especially methods for DNA analysis, there's a practical need for law enforcement and the justice system to stay receptive to revisiting older cases as new technologies emerge.

After the gut punch of not being believed when she initially came forward as a victim of rape, and having her harrowing experience become entangled in the press over a firestorm of misinformation, Jane Doe's life took a turn she never anticipated. For years, she carried not only the weight of the assault itself but also the burden of being labeled a liar in the court of public opinion. The disbelief and accusation likely touched every area of her life, having far-reaching effects, and potentially influencing her relationships, career opportunities, and mental health.

There came a day in late 2017 when I spoke with her myself with a commitment to solve her case. This conversation marked a turning point, not just in the investigation but in Jane Doe's long journey toward healing and justice. The prospect of reopening the case after so many years brought with it a mix of hope and trepidation for Jane Doe, who had learned to live with the unresolved nature of her assault.

In our first conversation by phone, Jane burst into tears and wept openly, saying, "I had a premonition I was going to get a phone call about this case." Her response underscored the profound impact that the unresolved case had on her life. Even after more than two decades, the memory of the assault and the subsequent public ordeal remained vivid, demonstrating how unresolved cases can continue to haunt survivors, affecting their daily lives and emotional well-being long after the immediate events have passed.

What would happen over the next two months would deliver a measure of validation that had eluded her for over two decades, illustrating how the significant advancements in DNA analysis that have occurred since Jane Doe's initial case represents a powerful tool for justice, offering hope to survivors like Jane who have long lived without resolution. Reinvestigating the case using advanced DNA analysis techniques offered the prospect of closure.

Her Special Victims Cold Case would be solved, marking a significant victory not just for Jane Doe personally but for the broader cause of justice for sexual assault survivors. The resolution of her case sent a powerful message about the importance of perseverance in seeking justice, the value of advances in forensic science, and the need for law enforcement and media to approach sexual assault cases with sensitivity and thoroughness. The potential for scientific advancements to correct past injustices and provide long-overdue answers to survivors and their families is a testament to the value of revisiting cold cases. For Jane, what was formerly a miscarriage of justice would finally be rectified, exemplifying that the truth can be affirmed even after many years. Though Jane should never have had to deal with the stigmatization of the media debacle, as a result of the police mishandling her investigation, knowing justice would prevail on the far side of her suffering may well have made the overwhelming opposition she faced more bearable.

Chapter 3

A STRANGER RAPE IN PROSPECT PARK

April 26, 1994

For those residing in Brooklyn, the mid-1990s brought with it a cautious optimism that the crime rate, which had peaked in the earlier part of the decade, was declining. The crack epidemic, which had ravaged communities and fueled much of the violent crime, was finally waning. As a result, there was a noticeable decrease in violent crime overall, bringing a sense of relief to many neighborhoods that had been hard hit. For Brooklyn residents who had long lived under the shadow of high crime rates, there was a tangible uptick in the quality of their day-to-day lives.

As of April 1994, New York City was experiencing a promising trend, with crime rates declining for the fifth consecutive month. This downward trajectory was a source of hope for city officials and residents alike, signaling that better policing strategies implemented to combat crime were beginning to yield positive results. This multi-month reduction in the overall crime rates was indicative of a longer-term trend toward improved public safety which was attributed to several factors following the crack epidemic. The implementation of CompStat, a police management system that went online in 1994, as well as economic improvements and community-based initiatives contributed to the overall reduction in criminal activity. While some areas continued to struggle, many Brooklyn neighborhoods that had once been synonymous with high crime rates were starting to see visible improvements.

Places like Prospect Park, a sprawling 526-acre public space that shares its borders with five densely populated Brooklyn neighborhoods—Park

Slope, Prospect Heights, Prospect Lefferts Gardens, Flatbush, and Windsor Terrace—remained a popular gathering place where people could enjoy a wide array of activities. From birdwatching enthusiasts to avid cyclists, the park continued to serve as a vital green space in the urban landscape. This expansive park, with its diverse ecosystems and recreational facilities, provided a much-needed respite from the concrete jungle of New York City, offering residents and visitors alike a place outdoors to connect with nature and with each other.

Though crime in Prospect Park was down, consistent with the overall trend in the city, it was not entirely without incidents. In the twelve months leading up to Jane Doe's rape, there was one homicide on record, one completed forcible rape, and another attempted rape. Considering the park's size and the number of visitors it attracted daily, these incidents were relatively few.

During the warmer months, when park usage typically peaked, the police presence of patrolling officers was redoubled. This increased vigilance was a response to the fact that crimes are more likely to happen during this time of year due to increased opportunities for predation.[1] The heightened police presence was intended to reassure park-goers that Prospect Park was safe.

No one who routinely spent time in the scenic park wanted to fathom the idea that lurking within this well-frequented community enclave would be a sexual predator, who having just been released from prison as a parolee for prior sex crimes, could be scouting his next victim. A chilling thought that challenges the well-kempt perception of the park as a safe haven easily confronts the complexities of urban life.

The reporting of rape in the park in the middle of the day would certainly stoke fears, shaking the community's perception that their local officers on patrol were keeping them safe. This kind of news would have the potential of decreased usage and a heightened sense of vulnerability among regular visitors, drawing to mind comparisons to the crimes in similar settings, such as the Central Park jogger who was ruthlessly raped in April of 1989, just five years earlier. That high-profile case shocked the city and the nation, leaving a lasting impact on public consciousness and perceptions of safety in urban parks.

When it comes to sex crimes like forcible rape, the body is the crime scene. Unlike victims of homicide where the deceased body is taken to the Medical Examiner's office for an autopsy following the investigation by the ME at the scene, collecting forensic evidence from a living person requires a vastly different approach. The process of gathering crucial evidence such as semen, saliva, blood samples, hair fibers, and skin cells from the body of a sexual assault survivor demands not only technical expertise but also a high degree of empathy and sensitivity.

Collecting timely evidence is crucial for rape convictions; the window for collecting certain types of evidence can be quite narrow, making the prompt and proper collection of samples essential to the investigative process. Unlike a static crime scene, the human body is dynamic, and evidence can be lost or degraded quickly. Professionals, such as forensic nurses, are trained not only in proper evidence collection techniques but also in trauma-informed care to ensure that a survivor feels safe and supported throughout the examination. These professionals often serve as a bridge between the medical and legal aspects of the case, ensuring that evidence is collected properly while providing immediate medical care.

The Sexual Offense Evidence Collection Kit, often abbreviated to the more generic moniker of "rape kit" or "vitullo kit," remains an important way to standardize collection methods and to ensure a proper chain of custody. These kits play a vital role in solving and prosecuting rape cases, providing a systematic approach to gathering and preserving evidence that can withstand scrutiny in court. Forensic examination is a comprehensive process that involves documenting injuries, collecting biological samples, and preserving any physical evidence that may be present on the survivor's body or clothing. This evidence could be crucial to identifying a perpetrator, corroborating a survivor's account, and potentially linking the assailant to other crimes. Proper handling, storage, and analysis of the collected samples are critical to maintaining the integrity of the evidence for potential legal proceedings.

The development and implementation of standardized rape kits represent a significant advancement in the investigation of sexual assaults. In the late 1970s, at a time when there was a large cultural stigma that colored the care survivors of sexual assault received, Martha Goddard, an activist and a sexual assault survivor herself, is credited with introducing the first generation of rape kits in Chicago area hospitals. This innovation proved to efficiently streamline investigations, providing a more consistent and thorough approach to evidence collection. Goddard's efforts spurred positive change; there was a shift in the paradigm of how these crimes were investigated and how survivors were treated in the immediate aftermath of an assault.

By the time I got to Special Victims, the generally accepted practice was that if the rape kit comes back negative, for lack of usable forensic evidence, the clothing worn by the rape survivor could also be tested. Unfortunately, this practice was rarely adopted throughout the mid-1990s, and most often it was only the rape kit, and rarely the clothing, that would be sent to the lab. The failure to consistently test clothing was a missed opportunity, potentially leaving valuable evidence unexplored in many investigations, as these items can often yield crucial DNA evidence or other forensic clues that might not be captured in the standard rape kit examination.

Before solving Jane Doe's case, I'd spent a significant amount of time working on rape kit backlog cases, with the objective of reopening those cases that had forensic value and were still within the statute of limitations to be able to prosecute. For many detectives working on sex crimes, it is common knowledge that there used to be a heavy backlog of rape kits throughout the United States. This backlog was primarily due to cost considerations related to testing and a general lack of manpower to dedicate to processing and testing the kits. The result was that many kits sat on shelves in storage, a system failure that was in dire need of reform. The backlog was also arguably a betrayal of survivors who had undergone invasive examinations with the expectation that the evidence would be used to pursue their cases.

The reasons for untested kits are multifaceted. In some cases, a kit may go untested because the rape survivor chooses not to work with law enforcement in reporting the crime. This highlights the complex personal decisions that survivors must navigate in the aftermath of an assault. The decision not to pursue a case can be influenced by a variety of factors, including fear of retaliation, lack of faith in the justice system, or the desire to avoid further trauma associated with a lengthy investigation or legal proceeding. Respecting the survivor's decision if she or he decides not to report or prosecute is just as supporting survivors who do choose to pursue justice.

As part of a nationwide advocacy effort to spark comprehensive legislation reform, a rape backlog initiative was funded by grants issued by the Manhattan District Attorney's Office.[2] This initiative was further supported through legislation signed by Governor Andrew Cuomo in November of 2016. These efforts represented a significant step forward in addressing the backlog issue, recognizing the importance of timely processing of rape kits. There was a growing recognition by legislators and others in public office that making strides with rape kit backlog was an essential facet of better criminal justice reform.

As of 2020, Illinois State Police instituted an online tracking system, giving survivors the ability to track when their rape kit is being processed at the forensic lab and when a report of the lab's findings are sent to law enforcement.[3] This innovative approach empowers survivors by providing increased transparency in the investigative process, resulting in a layer of systemic accountability. By allowing survivors to track the progress of their kit, it ensures that fewer kits fall through the cracks or remain untested for extended periods. What's being done statewide in Illinois serves as a model for other states looking to reduce their own backlogs.

While challenges remain, as a result of these and other initiatives, many states have been able to make significant headway in their testing efforts, ensuring that more perpetrators are brought to justice. This progress represents a crucial step toward a more just and effective response to sexual assault. However, better administration in testing rape kits is just one part of a larger system that needs ongoing reform to better serve survivors and hold perpetrators accountable.

The prevalence of this problem in a place like New York City, and other jurisdictions, can be a bleak fact of life for detectives and survivors alike, while perpetrators who may be repeat offenders elude capture in the short term. The impact of unsolved cases extends beyond the immediate victims, affecting the broader community's sense of safety. The psychological toll on a community living under the shadow of unsolved crimes can be profound, affecting everything from local businesses to community engagement.

Those who commit serial crimes often do so with the same modus operandi (MO). Serial rapists may have behaviors such as where and how they approach their victims, or the words they say to subdue and control them, that are consistent with their MO, which feasibly helps detectives to apprehend them. These behavioral signatures can be crucial in linking cases and building a profile of the offender, potentially leading to their identification and arrest. The ability to recognize and analyze these patterns requires not only skilled investigators but also data management systems that can track and identify similarities across multiple crime scenes and victims.

Unfortunately, when there is a crime wave and a high number of incidents, many stranger rape cases go unsolved. The sheer volume of cases can overwhelm even the most dedicated and skilled investigators, leading to a backlog that hampers timely and thorough investigations. The likelihood that crucial evidence may be lost or degraded goes up over time, and as cases pile up, the public's confidence in law enforcement's ability to protect them may wane.

There is a critical window of time when leads are freshest and evidence is most readily available. Momentum in the investigation of a stranger rape often slows down after two weeks have elapsed with no significant developments post-incident. If the trail grows cold, it will be increasingly difficult to solve the case. This diminishing window for success adds another stressor to already overburdened detectives, who must balance their responsibility for thorough investigation with the urgency to act on fresh leads. This challenge is further compounded by the fact that many victims may need time to process their trauma before feeling ready to fully engage with the investigation, potentially forestalling breaks in the case.

While there's pressure to solve a case, a detective is also expected to accept new assignments, giving time and attention to other cases as Special Victims Squads are often chronically overworked and inundated with new caseloads across cities and communities. This constant juggling act between active investigations and newly assigned cases creates a challenging environment where detectives must prioritize their efforts, often at the expense of older, unsolved cases. The need to divide their attention across multiple cases can lead to difficult decisions about which leads to pursue and which cases to temporarily shelve, potentially allowing perpetrators from older cases to escape detection and evade justice.

With Brooklyn being such a large borough with so much crime to keep up with, unsolved cases may close when it's decided, sometimes by higher-ups, that all leads have been exhausted. While prioritization is necessary given a division's limited resources, this decision can seem arbitrary to devastated victims and their families who may fear that their cases once closed may never again be reopened.

If criminal investigations took place in a vacuum, where every shred of evidence could be turned over and thoughtfully examined, and every lead could be thoroughly followed up on, without the real-world constraints of overtime bans, budget cutbacks, and burnout, inarguably, the percentage of crimes solved would be much higher. Undoubtedly, resource constraints have a real but unquantifiable and variable effect on the outcome of many criminal investigations.

For detectives, the intensity of Special Victims Division investigations may take their toll, as the emotional burden of working with sexual assault cases day in and day out can be overwhelming, leading to burnout, stress, fatigue, and even secondary traumatization. This psychological impact on detectives affects not only their personal well-being but also the quality and consistency of their work. Given the emotional gravity of their work, comprehensive support systems, regular counseling, and a healthy rotation of assignments and self-care strategies are strategies to help detectives better manage their caseloads.

When seasoned detectives move on to other assignments opting to serve on other squads or agencies, this turnover compounds the challenges faced by Special Victims Squads. The loss of experienced investigators means the loss of institutional knowledge, a disruption in long-standing or key community relationships, and the death of experienced talent with the unique set of investigative skills necessary for handling complex cases. The changeover could equate to delays in active investigations as detectives who may be more green strive to get up to speed, potentially impacting the outcomes of those investigations that require enhanced support.

According to RAINN,[4] the Rape, Abuse & Incest National Network, "only twenty-five out of every thousand perpetrators will end up in prison." That is a paltry 4 percent, a statistic that starkly illustrates the challenges in prosecuting and convicting perpetrators of sexual violence. This low rate of incarceration raises serious questions about the effectiveness of the criminal justice system in addressing sexual assault cases and providing justice for survivors. The statistical disparity between the incidental occurrence of sexual violence and the legal system's inability to convict as many perpetrators as are accountable for those incidents could plausibly contribute to a cycle of impunity that emboldens offenders and discourages victims from reporting.

RAINN also finds that "one in six American women has been the victim of an attempted or completed rape."[5] This shocking statistic indicates how prevalent violence against women is in the United States, highlighting a pervasive societal issue that affects millions of lives. The widespread nature of this problem underscores the urgent need for comprehensive strategies to prevent and address sexual violence while actively working on reforms in the criminal justice system to increase accountability for perpetrators.

Think how many women you have in your life, those who may make up your tribe of friends, family, work colleagues, and casual acquaintances. One in six of them is a victim of attempted or completed rape. This drives home the reality of sexual violence, and the prevalence of these experiences among women we know personally, impacting communities, families, and individuals across all walks of life.

If a New York jury convicts an alleged perpetrator of Rape One, which is a completed forcible rape, the minimum sentence is fifteen years. This substantial sentence reflects the severity with which the legal system views this crime, acknowledging the profound impact it has on victims. However, in light of low conviction rates, it's debatable whether the lengthy sentence is a deterrent to those who would commit future sex crimes. According to another data set compiled through RAINN, looking at Justice Department National Crime Victimization figures for sexual assault from 2010 to 2014, just 0.7 percent of reported rapes resulted in a felony conviction. This staggeringly low conviction rate highlights the significant gap between the legal consequences prescribed for rape and the actual outcomes in the justice system.

When comparing the pervasiveness of stranger rape to acquaintance rape, a lesser percentage of 15–20 percent of rape cases are committed by strangers, while more than 50 percent of both stranger and acquaintance rapes are going unreported. The high rate of unreported cases points to systemic issues that discourage victims from coming forward, such as fear, shame, or lack of faith in the justice system. More than half of the time, in stranger rapes, there is a weapon involved and injuries incurred, highlighting the often violent nature of these attacks. More than 90 percent of the perpetrators of stranger rapes are male, and over 90 percent of the victims of stranger rape are female. These gender-based statistics reflect broader patterns of sexual violence and highlight the gendered nature of this crime. While people of all genders can be both perpetrators and victims of sexual assault, statistics point to the need for targeted prevention efforts and a deeper examination of societal factors that contribute to male-perpetrated sexual violence against women.

Prosecution of rape cases hinges on survivors of sexual assault being brave enough to come forward with reporting that a sex crime has taken place. This initial step of reporting is often one of the most challenging for survivors as it requires them to confront their trauma and potentially face skepticism or disbelief from others. The decision to report is often accompanied by the fear of retaliation, shame, self-blame, and many other concerns about the impact reporting would have on one's personal and professional life.

Undergoing repeated police interviews throughout the course of an investigation requires courage and resilience, as survivors recount their traumatic experiences multiple times. These interviews, while necessary for gathering evidence and building a case, can be emotionally draining and re-traumatizing for survivors.

When the case goes to trial, the survivor may take the stand under oath, a process that can be emotionally taxing and potentially re-traumatizing, posing a significant challenge in their pursuit of justice. Subject to harsh cross-examination that attempts to tear down the survivor's credibility, probing into the survivor's past, and scrutinizing actions that were or weren't taken leading up to and after the crime, as well as restaging the day of the crime would be taxing for even the most stoic of survivors. Defense attorneys may employ aggressive tactics to discredit the survivor's testimony, focusing on irrelevant details or past behaviors that have no bearing on the assault itself. The proximity to the perpetrator in court requires survivors to face their attacker, often for the first time since the assault, which is likely highly triggering. Complex traumatic responses, including freeze responses, memory fragmentation, and delayed reporting might be used by the defense to cast doubt on the survivor's account, further compounding their distress and potentially influencing the outcome of the trial. The lengthy duration of legal proceedings can stretch on for months or even years and during this time survivors may struggle to move forward with their lives, feeling trapped in a state of limbo as they await resolution. The uncertainty of the outcome and the potential for a not-guilty verdict can be a source of significant anxiety, hindering their own recovery.

Community leaders, grassroots activists, and change agents who spearheaded the feminist movement reshaped societal beliefs around rape culture in the sixties and seventies and helped to usher in progressive change. These pioneers in the anti-rape movement played a crucial role in challenging long-standing myths and misconceptions about sexual violence. Their tireless efforts laid the groundwork for a fundamental shift in how society understood and responded to sexual assault, paving the way for significant legal and social reforms that continue to evolve today.

The stigmatizing belief that rape was an outcome of a woman "wanting it" or "asking for it," a narrative that was often unchallenged due to the shame-based silence of sexual assault victims, was taken back and recontextualized when survivors reclaimed their voices and began channeling their outrage into activism and advocacy.[6] The lie fell away and rape was seen in its true context, as an act of violence and power, rather than a crime of passion, debunking myths that rape was motivated by anything other than the insidious exercise of power and control. This shift in narrative was pivotal in changing public perception and policy around sexual violence. Given the hostile reception they often faced from both institutions and individuals invested in maintaining the status quo, the courage of these early activists, and survivors, was remarkable in confronting deeply entrenched societal attitudes, igniting the conversation around consent.

These feminist activists who led the charge in the anti-rape movement also contributed to significant legal reforms, effectively lobbying for changes in laws that previously made it difficult to prosecute rape cases, such as the admissibility of a victim's sexual history in court. These efforts led to the passage of rape shield laws in many states, protecting victims from invasive questioning that might prejudice the jury about their past sexual behavior during trials.

Beyond the scope of legal proceedings, survivors who were beginning to speak out challenged victim-blaming attitudes and also provided crucial firsthand accounts that informed better support services and legal responses, bringing the issue of sexual violence out of the shadows and into the forefront of public discourse. Their legacy can be seen in contemporary movements like #MeToo, which has further amplified survivor voices, transforming personal trauma into a powerful catalyst for social change. By sharing their experiences, survivors humanized the statistics.

The perpetrator who sexually assaulted Jane Doe, while she was crossing through Prospect Park on her way home following an ordinary grocery run, was never identified during the time Brooklyn detectives were actively working the case in April of 1994 through January of 1995. This nine-month period of active investigation would prove frustrating for both the detectives and Jane Doe, as leads were pursued but ultimately failed to yield a suspect. Intending to return to her home at the intersection of Prospect Place and Flatbush Avenue, Jane Doe veered off the well-trodden footpath along the lake onto a dirt bridle path alongside West Lake Drive, at 16:00 hours, on April 26, 1994, venturing toward a scenic, elevated area commonly known as Lookout Hill. The time of day, still daylight, likely gave Jane Doe a false sense of security. While walking with her grocery bags in hand through a wooded area, she heard something behind her and turned to see a male of medium build with a cane or walking stick trailing about twenty-five feet behind her. Turning back around, she was quickly encroached by this stranger who placed an arm around her neck in a chokehold warning her to be quiet and do as she was told, the rapid escalation underscoring the sudden and violent nature of the physical attack.

Feeling faint and seeing gold stars from a tight squeeze on her throat, she felt herself falling to her knees and fainting. When she came to, the man ordered her to walk further up the hillside, correcting media accounts that she'd been dragged up the hill. When she struggled, he told Jane Doe that he would "get the knife" though no weapon was ever observed. The threat of a weapon, even if not seen, served as a powerful tool of intimidation, illustrating the tactics employed by the attacker to maintain control over Jane. After physical force has been applied to subdue any resistance, this sort of fear tactic is commonly used by assailants to ensure their victims' compliance.

Getting her to a more secluded area on the hill, near a hollowed-out tree, standing behind her, he pulled her sweatshirt over her head, obscuring her eyesight. This action not only disoriented Jane but also potentially prevented her from seeing her attacker clearly, suggesting the rapist's premeditation, though she would later describe him accurately for a forensic artist who created a sketch capturing his likeness. Ordering her to turn around, Jane Doe's rapist guided her hand to his genitalia and commanded her to fondle it. Pulling Jane Doe's running shorts down, while she was still standing, he ordered her to take one leg out and then instructed her to lie down on the ground, atop his black army fatigue jacket, before forcibly raping Jane Doe with penis to vaginal penetration for a brief period of nonconsensual intercourse. The attack happened in broad daylight when Jane Doe was twenty-seven years old. Her rapist's brazenness in committing a felony sex assault in a public park during daylight hours suggests he's desensitized himself to any deterring aspects of being caught and prosecuted.

After her assailant had fled the crime scene, Jane Doe, who was crying, proceeded down the hill, and when a tearful plea for assistance went ignored by onlookers, she looked for a pay phone by the 16th Street exit. She soon spotted an officer of the Brooklyn South Task Force who was on radio motor patrol. She informed the Lieutenant that she'd been raped. An ambulance was called and Jane Doe was transported to Methodist Hospital at 20:15 hours to be interviewed by the Lead Detective, Det. Andrea Sorrentino, who was part of a specialty squad that handled crimes such as first-degree rape, criminal sexual acts, and sexual abuse cases. Dr. Fauzia, the physician who conducted the initial medical exam on Jane Doe remarked the inside of the vaginal wall seemed tender though there was no vaginal tearing. Of course, it was understood by both detective and physician alike that the absence of visible tearing did not invalidate the fact that a sexual assault had occurred.

Because many survivors are traumatized in the immediate aftermath of a sexual assault, according to sex crimes investigators, it's not at all unusual for it to take up to several interviews before a full recollection of the crime can be pieced together. This understanding of the impact of trauma on memory acknowledges that the process of gathering a complete and accurate account of the assault will require multiple conversations over time, allowing the survivor to process their experience and recall details that may initially be unclear or fragmented.

During a traumatic experience, the body is adrenalized as the sympathetic nervous system activates a fight-or-flight response. This physiological reaction to extreme stress can significantly affect how memories are formed and stored. Much of the processing that would normally take place in the formation of memories is suspended as the body responds to distress experienced at the subcortical level. This neurobiological perspective helps explain why survivors may have difficulty providing a coherent narrative immediately after an assault. A flood of stress hormones, namely cortisol and adrenaline, can interfere with the normal functioning of the hippocampus, a region of the brain essential for memory formation and consolidation.

The impact of trauma on memory formation and recall is a complex process that involves various parts of the brain. The heightened state of arousal during a traumatic event can lead to vivid memories of certain sensory details while other aspects of the experience may be poorly encoded or difficult to access. This phenomenon, often referred to as "trauma-induced amnesia" or "dissociative amnesia," is a protective mechanism that can shield the individual from overwhelming emotional distress.

Understanding the neurobiology of trauma and how it can impact a survivor's ability to provide a linear or complete account of the assault immediately after the event is crucial for investigators and professionals working with sexual assault survivors, as it informs how to approach interviews and how to interpret inconsistencies or gaps in a survivor's initial account. While sometimes a victim will withhold information due to being afraid of what may come of being completely candid, having this essential neurobiological context to trauma helps investigators avoid making premature judgments.

Many survivors of sexual assault experience a range of trauma responses from dissociation to excruciating shame to emotional numbing. These reactions are normal responses to abnormal and traumatic events, serving as coping mechanisms that allow the individual to navigate the immediate aftermath of the assault. Dissociation manifests as a feeling of detachment from one's body or surroundings, which may affect how the survivor perceives and later recalls the events. Memories can feel fragmented or dreamlike, making it challenging for survivors to provide a coherent narrative of what they experienced. Shame, a common emotional response, and very corrosive, can lead survivors to withhold certain details of the assault out of fear of judgment or blame though they are in a supportive environment. Emotional numbing, another protective response, and a coping mechanism may result in a flat affect that could be misinterpreted by investigators as a lack of credibility by those unfamiliar with trauma responses. That's why educating investigators and other professionals about these varied trauma responses is essential.

With enough rest and time, details of memories that were initially fragmented may give rise to more consistent recollections of the assault. This gradual process of memory consolidation and retrieval underscores the importance of exercising patience in the investigative process as the survivor's own testimony and recollection of events are vital components of the investigation. Over time, the brain will naturally integrate traumatic memories, offering a more complete narrative of the day of the assault.

Detectives like Sorrentino are confronting victims when they are at their most vulnerable, and oftentimes a verbal promise to do one's best provides a modicum of confidence for the aggrieved that justice will be served. Offering reassurance paired with skill, empathy, and an understanding of trauma-informed practices can be crucial in establishing trust. A positive initial interaction between a detective and a survivor can set the tone for the entire investigation, significantly influencing the survivor's personal resolve to cooperate with investigators or to prosecute in the time after a perpetrator has been charged.

During the first interview, Jane Doe mentioned there was a rally planned in Prospect Park that upcoming weekend, and then Jane added, off the cuff, "Maybe I should show up there and say something." This remark, an informational fragment devoid of its full context, made during a traumatic and emotionally charged situation, would later take on unintended significance and unforeseen consequences. Jane's words were included in Detective Sorrentino's case notes and she submitted DD5, the detective's formal write-up. Unfortunately, it was this casual isolated remark that was misconstrued as those higher-ups in the police department found cause for questioning the survivor's credibility and casting doubt on her personal account.

In most cases such as this one, the immediacy of the victim's outcry, along with a detailed description of what took place, is often reason enough to believe the victim's account is credible.

Jane's remark, likely sparked by the feeling of anger following incredulity and shock, was perhaps her attempt to reclaim some agency and to process her experience. Perhaps it was an attempt to build a rapport with the detective who would be handling her investigation. In the aftermath of an assault, when feeling acutely victimized, it's common for survivors to want to regain some measure of control over their narrative.

Jane Doe could not have predicted that she would be publicly branded as someone vying for personal gain through allegations of rape. This unfortunate outcome underscores the potential for survivors' words and actions to be misconstrued, particularly when taken out of context or viewed through a lens of skepticism. In his first column about the park rape, which ran under the dual headlines of "Rape hoax the real crime" and "Enough crime without inventing it," McAlary, who identified Jane Doe as twenty-seven years old and Black, also put Jane Doe's sexual orientation as a lesbian on blast when he postulated, "The woman, who will probably end up being arrested herself, invented the crime, they said, to promote her rally."[7] This community gathering he referred to as "her" rally was sponsored by the Gay and Lesbian Anti-Violence Project. Despite it being organized by a larger community-based group, the use of the personal pronoun attempts to portray Jane Doe as someone with a personal agenda to advance. While he should know better, he shows little understanding that community-based initiatives are collective by nature. McAlary's inflammatory statement not only questioned the veracity of Jane Doe's assault claim but framed aspects of her identity as somehow relevant to the credibility of her claim, playing into harmful stereotypes and biases. His assertion that she would "probably end up being arrested herself" went beyond skepticism and into the realm of accusation, suggesting that law enforcement shared his doubts about her story.

While Matt Foreman, the Executive Director of the AVP, said the rally, an event planned far in advance, did not formally have Jane Doe scheduled to appear as a featured speaker, Foreman made it clear he had no objections to her making some informal comments if she decided to attend.[8] Stating his position, Foreman corrects for the record that McAlary's portrayal of Jane Doe in his columns as a publicity hound who's willing to act in bad faith in order to draw attention is untrue. McAlary's characterization of the rally as "her" event misleadingly implied that Jane Doe had a central role in its organization or that it was somehow orchestrated in response to her assault. In reality, as Foreman clarified, the rally was a pre-planned event by the AVP, and not specifically tied to Jane Doe's case, discrediting McAlary's implication that Jane had engineered a premeditated publicity stunt in order to promote "her" rally. The AVP's long-standing commitment to addressing violence against LGBTQ individuals was unfairly overshadowed by the controversy surrounding Jane Doe's case, detracting from the mission of an organization that existed entirely independently of Jane Doe's individual case.

Jane Doe's remark to Sorrentino about maybe showing up at the event and saying something, an outcome which did not come to pass, was twisted into McAlary writing in his column, "She promised yesterday to deliver a first-person speech on her own rape." Then, in his final column written as a follow-up to this story, he wrote, "She delivered her statement, as promised, to the rally. The alleged victim got more publicity than she dreamed about."[9] Though a statement she'd written was read aloud, she did not attend, and this bawdy misappropriation of Detective Sorrentino's notes in the DD5 police form she submitted, which McAlary was likely not privy to reviewing firsthand, was instead printed from information received second-hand, from an unnamed source.

McAlary's semantic elevation of Jane Doe's casual offhand comment into a "promise" to deliver a speech represents a significant distortion of the facts. His subsequent claim that she had fulfilled this nonexistent promise and received extensive publicity further compounds the misrepresentation. The reality that Jane Doe did not attend the rally and that only a written statement was read on her behalf starkly contrasts with McAlary's portrayal of events, which significantly distorted the facts. McAlary's decision to reinforce a false narrative created more harm by fueling suspicions about Jane Doe's motive for reporting her assault.

To recap—a woman who is a Black lesbian alleges she was raped. This incident, occurring in the mid-1990s, immediately highlights the intersectionality of race, gender, and sexual orientation in how sexual assault cases were perceived and handled. The public scrutiny to which Jane was exposed cannot be fully understood by examining each aspect of her identity in isolation but instead requires special consideration of how these identities intersected to compound her vulnerability in light of the violent assault.

It's not beyond the pale of plausibility to assert that in the mid-1990s there was a baked-in bias against readily believing truth claims made by a Black, lesbian, woman of color whose suffering McAlary subconsciously or consciously capitalized on because he felt he could. This assertion points to the deeply entrenched societal biases that exist and continue to exist against individuals who occupy multiple marginalized identities. The intense skepticism and disbelief Jane Doe faced can be seen as a consequence of intersectional oppression, where her credibility was questioned not just because she was a woman alleging rape but because she was specifically a Black lesbian woman making such a claim.

This points to deep-rooted systemic biases that have long influenced how stories are reported and how different voices are valued in society. As a member of the press, McAlary's perpetuation of these biases in his portrayal of Jane and Jane's claim demonstrates how journalists can reinforce existing power structures and further marginalize those who are already vulnerable individuals.

McAlary's position as a white male journalist with access to police sources gave him a platform and credibility that the victim, given her marginalized identities as a Black woman and as a lesbian, may not have been afforded. This imbalanced power dynamic illustrates intersectional privilege, where McAlary's multiple privileged identities as a white, cis-gendered, heterosexual man intersect to grant him both authority and credibility in the public sphere. In contrast, Jane Doe's intersecting marginalized identities contributed to her being perceived as less credible or worthy of belief.

The case also highlights the importance of considering how different systems of oppression—racism, sexism, homophobia—interact and reinforce each other in cases of sexual violence. Jane Doe's experience as a survivor was inevitably shaped by her racial identity, her gender, and her sexual orientation. Each aspect potentially influenced how she was treated by law enforcement, portrayed by McAlary in his column, and perceived by the public as a result of his platform writing for a well-known tabloid newspaper. This intersectional perspective is crucial for understanding the full scope of challenges faced by Jane Doe, who belonged to multiple marginalized groups.

Those who know what it is to be marginalized may observe with collective relief that the needle calibrating our cultural progression is moving in the direction of a more equitable and just society. This sentiment reflects the gradual shifts in societal attitudes and institutional practices that have occurred since the 1990s, particularly in areas of racial justice, LGBTQIA+ rights, and the treatment of sexual assault survivors. The progress made in these areas, while not complete or uniformly applied, represents significant strides toward greater recognition and protection of marginalized communities. It acknowledges the tireless efforts of activists and allies who have worked to challenge systemic biases and push for meaningful change.

Following Sorrentino's initial interview with Jane Doe on April 26, 1994, the day of the attack, back at police headquarters, Deputy Commissioner for Public Information John Miller, requested an evening briefing on the case, and was said to have asked Detective Sorrentino, skeptically, "Are you sure this is legit?" Miller's skeptical question shows the immediate scrutiny Jane's sexual assault case faced, even within law enforcement circles. While Miller was a high-ranking official within the police department, his skepticism may be attributed in part to never having received comprehensive training on sexual assault investigations. Perhaps because his position as Deputy Commissioner of Public Information may never have warranted such specialized training, there may have been some ignorance driving his doubts.

With a touch of subtlety, out of deference for her superior officer, Sorrentino tried to convey to Miller that it was too soon in the arc of the investigation to presume Jane Doe's account wasn't on the level. Her reluctance to make hasty judgments demonstrated a commitment to due process and fair treatment of the victim. Sorrentino's measured response reflected strong professional instincts and a victim-centered approach to Jane's sexual assault investigation. By resisting the pressure to make an immediate judgment, or further indulge Miller's skepticism, she exemplified the importance of thorough, unbiased investigative practices.

It was too early to make a judgment call on what had taken place just a few hours earlier as the facts about the assault were still coming in. Rushing to judgment based on preliminary information, the accuracy of which may be limited, affected by trauma, and subject to change as more evidence is collected would be foolhardy. There was plenty of due diligence, such as analyzing the findings of the collected biological and physical evidence, that needed to be done before any solid conclusions about Jane's sexual assault case could be drawn.

Careful, methodical investigation is crucial in ensuring justice for victims and maintaining the integrity of the legal process. So, it came as a shocker for Sorrentino to walk into work the morning of April 28th, three days into the investigation, and come face-to-face with an angry sergeant upset with Sorrentino for leaking the case to the press. Of course, Sorrentino hadn't sabotaged the case of her own accord, and the sudden white-hot speculation around the veracity of Jane Doe's case added a heap of pressure to get the case solved as public scrutiny mounted.

The media attention debating the validity of Jane's rape claim likely created a challenging environment for conducting a thorough and unbiased investigation, potentially diverting resources and attention from the process of gathering evidence. Without the glare of scrutiny, there's no saying how the investigation would have progressed or unfolded, perhaps differently had Jane Doe been believed and granted the privacy she deserved without the pressure of public speculation and premature judgments.

As the controversy played out, rather than pull Andrea Sorrentino off the case, making it seem as if the NYPD was engaged in a cover-up, the brass decided to keep Sorrentino, whom Jane Doe trusted, instated as the lead detective. This decision skillfully controlled optics and balanced public relations with the practical aspects of the investigation. The identity of McAlary's source would remain shrouded in a veil of secrecy. As a member of the press, McAlary was working with the benefit of a shield law in place, which varies by jurisdiction and state, but which in large part allows journalists, including columnists, the privilege of protecting their sources. This legal protection was originally intended to protect sources who were, for example, whistleblowers, so there was a way to get information to a member of the press. However, McAlary's unidentified source potentially hampered efforts to address the internal leaks and maintain the confidentiality of the investigation.

The first twenty-four hours following the sexual assault would have investigators back at the park for a cognitive reenactment pointing out the route Jane Doe traveled, canvassing the area, and talking to potential witnesses during an era when resources like video camera footage that might lead to a rapid arrest weren't nearly as prevalent as they are today. This initial phase of the investigation was crucial in gathering time-sensitive information that could lead to identifying and apprehending the perpetrator. Cognitive reenactment, a technique used to help victims recall details by revisiting the scene, could potentially uncover information that might have been overlooked in the immediate aftermath of the trauma, helping detectives to piece together a comprehensive picture of the events surrounding the assault.

On a hunch that Jane Doe's perpetrator may have been homeless, there was weekly scouring of the park surveillance footage from April 1994 through the months afterward as the investigation ensued but this led to few developments. Jane Doe's description of her assailant as a Black male, about six feet in height, of medium build, looking to be about thirty-five to forty-five years old, with dark matted hair, wearing a red shirt and a brown hat with a short brim was a critical step in the investigation that could be used in the search by members of law enforcement. While justice for Jane Doe would be deferred by a stretch of many years, her assailant would later be convicted for sexual assaults against other women in the time after the rape in Prospect Park. Based on the description, Lead Detective Andrea Sorrentino and other officers had a starting point for stopping and questioning people based on those who fit the description, though, to Jane Doe's dismay, some Black men who didn't fit the description of her assailant were being stopped by police officers anyway, raising issues around racial profiling.

There was one individual who was a very close physical match to the sketch Jane Doe provided, and there was the fleeting hope of nabbing the perpetrator sooner rather than later, but when this fellow was added to a lineup, it turned out it wasn't him. Jane Doe also reviewed approximately ten photo arrays of possible suspects, but nothing stood out to her. Without a concrete determination of the criminal's profile, questions such as whether this was a first strike, on the part of the offender, or a serial offense were still up in the air. This uncertainty about the offender's criminal history presented challenges for investigators as understanding whether they were dealing with a first-time offender or a serial rapist could greatly influence the direction of the investigation and the resources allocated to it.

The complexity of sexual assault cases, particularly those involving strangers, often presents unique challenges to investigators. Physical evidence can be nonexistent, scarce, or degraded, witness accounts may be limited, and the traumatic nature of the crime can affect the victim's ability to provide detailed information. The best approach is a thorough one in which investigators keep an open mind and look into all potential prospects, as more evidence gradually comes to light. This methodical approach requires patience, diligence, and a willingness to pursue multiple lines of inquiry, crucial to ensuring that no potential leads are overlooked. The misconstrued information from Detective Sorrentino's initial report played out in such a public way that the public scrutiny likely distracted her investigative efforts to close in on the rapist. This public mishandling of sensitive information highlights how McAlary's columns did not help and may have hobbled the investigation's progress.

Without a lot of concrete evidence to propel an investigation, it is often the depth of experience and a finely honed intuition that is the hallmark of good detective work integral to police work in the 1990s. Being able to read or gauge the way something is said, gleaning what's communicated nonverbally in eye-to-eye contact, and reviewing interrelated facts that appear at first glance to have no common thread is where the clues of a case reside. Interviews with witnesses and with persons of interest vetted through warm leads and incoming tips, as well as stopping and questioning individuals with a basis for reasonable suspicion, were traditional investigative pathways to be explored in Sorrentino's time. These tried and true methods, while time-consuming and sometimes yielding limited results, remained fundamental to thorough police work. The importance of community cooperation in these traditional methods cannot be overstated. Witnesses coming forward, community members providing tips, and the general public's willingness to assist law enforcement can often make a difference in solving complex cases.

Detective Sorrentino, who maintained an easy rapport with Jane Doe after having earned her trust, was acknowledged by Jane for working tirelessly on her behalf, even as Jane continued to feel stigmatized by the press, and at the mercy of those she felt were manipulating the details of her case for their own ends. Sorrentino's dedicated and empathetic approach provided a lifeline for Jane Doe during an incredibly challenging time, demonstrating the positive impact that an investigator can have on a victim's experience with the criminal justice system.

Chapter 4

SEMEN FOUND, NOT SPERM

In the time after Jane Doe's case closed, still unsolved, and after all leads were exhausted in January of 1995, it wasn't until the NYPD Rape Kit Backlog Project was underway that a DNA sample from Jane Doe's original vaginal swab was sent to a contracted lab called GeneScreen for retesting on September 24, 2001, six-and-a-half years after the original crime. This significant delay in DNA testing highlights the challenges faced by law enforcement and forensic labs in processing sexual assault evidence in a timely manner despite the fact that DNA technology was a game-changer, allowing for the identification of perpetrators with unprecedented accuracy. The backlog of untested rape kits has been a persistent issue across many jurisdictions, often leaving victims without closure and potentially allowing perpetrators to remain unidentified and at large.

There are any number of factors as to why rape kits from the early to mid-1990s were not consistently tested for DNA in the immediate aftermath of their crimes including lack of funding and staffing to support the crime labs, poorly collected or degraded samples, to lack of uniform protocols regarding how to prioritize which kits will be tested. CODIS, the national database managed by the FBI that would match DNA evidence to existing profiles, was not fully online until 1998. The implementation of CODIS marked a significant advancement in forensic technology, providing a powerful tool for linking DNA evidence across different cases and jurisdictions. However, its delayed availability and the lack of a fully operational national DNA database in 1994 and prior meant that many earlier cases, like Jane Doe's, did not benefit from this resource until years after the initial investigation.

The finding that a vaginal swab from Jane Doe's kit was negative for the presence of spermatozoa was consistent with what the original police lab, NYPD's then Scientific Research Division, had determined in 1994. This consistency in findings across different time periods and labs validates the initial forensic work, despite the lack of DNA analysis at the time. It wasn't until 2001 that any DNA analysis was completed on Jane's rape kit, highlighting the evolving nature of forensic technology and its application to cold cases.

According to a 1994 article by the *New York Post*'s Criminal Justice editor, Murray Weiss,[1] findings at the police lab by chemist Thomas Hickey in his lab report No. 94-2035, released on April 29, 1994, three days after the attack, confirmed the presence of the P30 antigen. This enzyme is present in human seminal plasma and was extracted from the victim's vaginal swab and running shorts. The detection of the P30 antigen provided crucial physical evidence supporting Jane Doe's account of the assault, even in the absence of spermatozoa. On the same day, April 29th, Police Commissioner William Bratton offered an apology for the department's haste, though the finer points about semen and lab findings were left out of his remarks. Bratton's apology, while addressing the department's initial mishandling of the case, notably omitted the scientific evidence that supported Jane Doe's claims.

Dr. Howard Baum, a forensic biologist at the city Medical Examiner's office, also independently corroborated Hickey's findings soon after being contacted by NYPD on May 10th[2] and consulted with Brooklyn special victims detectives on the internal report referencing Rape Case no. 624 for Jane Doe's Prospect Park attack. This secondary analysis by an independent expert provided crucial validation of the initial findings, strengthening the credibility of the forensic evidence.

The swab and shorts were positive for the antigen, as found earlier by the prior first-round lab results, and negative for spermatozoa, an indicator the male perpetrator was incapable of producing sperm perhaps due to a vasectomy or a medical condition such as azoospermia. This finding across multiple tests was significant because it confirmed the presence of seminal fluid, supporting Jane Doe's account of the assault. The finding of the absence of spermatozoa, provided important information about the perpetrator's biological characteristics, key to narrowing down potential suspects to a specific forensic profile.

In McAlary's third and final column related to the Prospect Park case, published with the headline "I'm right, but that's no reason to cheer," on page 6 on Friday, May 13, 1994, roughly two weeks after his prior two columns, McAlary reported there was no semen to support Jane Doe's claim. This assertion directly contradicted the forensic evidence that had been made public by this time, raising serious questions about McAlary's sources. McAlary cites that his unnamed sources in law enforcement, note the use of the plural, alluding to the possibility that there was more than one, who told him to, "Stand your ground. The lab is wrong."

When second-round lab findings were confirmed by May 10th, it's mind-boggling how McAlary could write, "At best, the lab reported the substance was saliva, male or female." This fallacious statement appears to be a deliberate misrepresentation of the scientific evidence. The confirmed presence of the P30 antigen, which is specific to seminal fluid, had been established by this point, making McAlary's claim about saliva particularly egregious. It leaves one wondering whether McAlary carelessly ran with printing misinformation or to what degree his police source left him hanging, and why, raises critical questions about the relationship between journalists and their sources.

Some are of the opinion that those in the police department had a vested interest in maintaining their multi-month streak of declining incidents of reported sex crimes and that "crunching the numbers" was a common practice to control the narrative. This suggests a systemic issue within law enforcement, where the pressure to show positive statistics could potentially lead to the manipulation of crime statistics, raising ethical concerns with far-reaching consequences for public safety and the mishandling of serious crimes.

The lead sentence of McAlary's May 13th column reads, "One morning you open the newspapers, and suddenly *you* are the story." This stylistic choice to write in the second person positions McAlary as both the narrator and the subject of his own story. He painted a sympathetic portrait of himself and patted himself on the back for having exercised restraint by not rushing to reply to the criticism coming his way when other journalists were publishing stories that corroborated the lab's finding of seminal fluid.

McAlary writes that editors stood behind his story and would not apologize for being right, though he told his police sources that he'd be willing to offer an apology to Jane Doe if he were in the wrong. The support from his editors, despite the conflicting evidence, raises questions about the editorial process and the newspaper's commitment to accuracy and accountability. McAlary's stated willingness to apologize if proven wrong seems at odds with his continued insistence on the veracity of his reporting, even as contradictory evidence mounted.

Then Managing Editor of the *New York Daily News*, Martin Gottlieb, who'd also worked at the *New York Times*, as well as the *Village Voice*, and was respected by peers for his competence and proficiency offered strong words of support from the outset, "Mike McAlary has a long track record of solid authoritative reporting, and we stand by his column." Staking the newspaper's reputation, this unequivocal endorsement from a seasoned journalist like Gottlieb lent significant credibility to McAlary's controversial reporting.

Daily News editor-in-chief Martin Dunn, who had come to the *Daily News* following a position at the *Boston Herald*, and who later had a second term as editor-in-chief of the *News* from 2003 to 2010, was more measured in his support and just before McAlary's third column was published, he stated, "I cannot comment on a report I have not personally seen or what it may or may not prove. Mike McAlary has written twice on the issue and we stand behind him." Dunn's more cautious and detached stance, while still supportive of McAlary, suggests an attempt to maintain some editorial distance from the controversy. This stance could be seen as an attempt to hedge against potential fallout if McAlary's reporting proved inaccurate. The editors' responses in this case likely influenced not only public perception of McAlary's reporting but also the internal dynamics of the newsroom.

These senior editors were ultimately responsible for ensuring that journalistic standards of accuracy and fairness were being met. Having never attempted to contact Jane Doe and in the rush to be first, McAlary's reliance on an unnamed police source made verifying the information prior to publication a difficult call for senior editors who would be the first to face intense scrutiny. The lack of transparency made it harder for editors to issue retractions for the errors in McAlary's columns, which made the tabloid vulnerable to legal action for the publication of defamatory content. It's unlikely the tabloid's legal team weighed in on the content of McAlary's columns before they were published. Had there been the luxury of time, without the pressures of a rapid news cycle, editors may have been able to convince McAlary to reconsider the tone of his first column, so as not to court controversy and to adhere better to editorial standards that wouldn't put the publication's reputation at stake.

Others on staff at the newspaper tabloid, twenty-five others, including crime reporter Jerry Capeci, who was critical of the protective stance taken by the editors of the *Daily News*, mounted a campaign in the form of a signed petition condemning McAlary's column as a disgrace.[3] This internal dissent within the newspaper highlights the ethical concerns raised by McAlary's reporting and the editorial decisions to support it. The fact that a significant number of staff members, including a respected crime reporter, felt compelled to formally protest McAlary's column underscores the controversial nature of his coverage and the divisions it created within the newsroom.

Escaping any professional disciplinary action, perhaps McAlary was motivated to continue covering the story after his first column caught the ire of community leaders because, in the tabloid business, fanning the flames of controversy, on a story he was first to break, could be good for business. This perspective suggests that McAlary's continued coverage may have been driven by commercial interests rather than journalistic integrity, highlighting the potential conflict between sensationalism and responsible reporting in tabloid journalism.

In addition, in the event that history was repeating itself and Jane Doe's allegations of rape turned out to be false, McAlary might be acknowledged for what would look like in hindsight as shrewd acumen in drawing a parallel to Tawana Brawley, a high-profile story from seven years earlier. The comparison to the Brawley case, which was highly controversial and divisive, demonstrates how past high-profile cases can influence the reporting and public perception of current events, sometimes to the detriment of truth and justice. Though Brawley was never convicted of criminal charges, McAlary wrote about Jane Doe, in his initial column, "The woman, who probably will wind up being arrested herself, invented the crime, they said, to promote her rally." This statement shows McAlary's willingness to make bold, potentially damaging claims about a rape victim based on limited information.

Writing a second and third column also gave McAlary the opportunity to defend his position in his chosen medium. This persistence in defending his stance, despite mounting evidence and criticism, reveals a reluctance to admit error or reconsider his initial reporting. Unfortunately, he seemed to have paid little mind to the possibility that whatever information he was getting from his police source may have been a derivative of the department's mishandling of a sexual assault case. This oversight highlights the risks of relying too heavily on a single source, which can lead to a narrow, biased, or one-sided perspective, particularly in sensitive cases where seeking out diverse sources, multiple perspectives, and thorough fact-checking should be de rigueur.

Any flaws in the interpretation of Detective Sorrentino's DD5, and any other documentation the detective submitted corroborating what Jane Doe recalled or said to her, would impact the information the source ultimately passed onto McAlary. This illustrates how errors or biases are often amplified as information passes through multiple parties. The chain of transmitted information transmission, from Jane Doe to Detective Sorrentino, from Sorrentino's documentation to the source, and from McAlary's police source to McAlary, provides multiple opportunities for misinterpretation, bias, and error to creep in.

Though McAlary may have been confident about the information he was receiving, because of who it came from within the NYPD, having a solid connection does not equate to receiving unbiased and objective information that is error-free. Even when dealing with seemingly reliable police sources, because of the source's position of authority within the police department, journalists need to maintain a critical perspective regardless of the perceived authority of the source in order to safeguard against the propagation of misinformation and biased narratives. Relationships that develop between journalists and law enforcement sources can result in mayhem when the desire to maintain insider access or trust in a source's reliability overrides the need to verify what's been shared. The fear of losing access to a valuable source or damaging a trusted relationship can sometimes lead journalists to accept information at face value without applying the same rigorous standards of verification they might use with less established sources.

In his last column, McAlary references the Monday before Friday the 13th, as the day, "A big detective boss told senior officials that the lab report was final: No semen found, period." Though the identity of the "detective boss" in McAlary's column goes unnamed, it's likely McAlary was referring to Chief of Detectives Joseph R. Borrelli. This reference to an unnamed high-ranking police official added a layer of complexity to the case, suggesting that misinformation or a misunderstanding of information may have originated from within the upper echelons of the NYPD.

Ten days after McAlary's May 13th column is published in the *New York Daily News*, Leonard Levitt, a staff writer with New York *Newsday*, publishes content on Monday, May 23rd,[4] correcting the official record, in light of recent developments in which, [Commissioner] "Bratton confirmed two lab reports were done, saying the second was necessary because Chief of Detectives Joe Borrelli was 'confused' by the medical jargon in the first." So much for, "No semen found, period." This correction by Levitt highlights the evolving nature of the case and the potential for misinterpretation of the scientific evidence. Bratton's admission of Borrelli's confusion underscores the importance of clear communication between forensic experts and law enforcement officials, especially in high-profile cases.

Detective Andrea Sorrentino recalls being pulled into an executive staff meeting with police brass which included Borrelli, Bratton, and Miller. The scrutiny surrounding the details of the case, and now the meeting with all three high-ranking officials, had her feeling more than a little nervous walking into the room that day. Though the exact date of this meeting isn't conclusive, it likely took place sometime between May 9th and May 23rd. Chief Joseph Borrelli, who'd made a name for himself after having captured the serial killer known as the Son of Sam back in August of 1977, was well known by those within the NYPD, and he and Sorrentino were already professional acquaintances.

Seeing her frustrated and personally embarrassed by how her investigation on behalf of Jane Doe had become such media fodder, Borrelli had reassuring words for the detective, telling Sorrentino that she had nothing to fear. This meeting, involving high-ranking officials and the lead detective, underscores the gravity with which the NYPD was now treating the case and its public fallout. Borrelli's reassurance to Sorrentino suggests an acknowledgment within the department that the handling of the case had been problematic.

Borrelli praised Commissioner Bratton for his kind temperament and congeniality, and when Sorrentino came face-to-face with Bratton, he greeted her by way of apology, first saying, "I'm sorry." At the meeting, Borrelli and Miller asked Sorrentino for clarification, asking her to give her account of the investigation still underway. Sorrentino recalls Bratton having told her, "Let me hear from you what happened." Sorrentino asserted that everything she knew was documented in the reports she submitted. This interaction reveals a more conciliatory approach from the top brass, with Bratton's apology suggesting a recognition of the mishandling of the case. The request for Sorrentino to provide her account directly indicates an attempt to get a clear, unfiltered understanding of the investigation, potentially to correct earlier instances of misinterpretation or miscommunication.

In Sorrentino's written reports, which were reviewed and signed off by a supervising sergeant, Andrea chose words to convey there was evidence of a seminal ejaculation, but that the emission wasn't capable of impregnation because of the absence of motile sperm within the seminal fluid. This had initially been a source of confusion for Borrelli, and the cause for another round of lab tests to be ordered and completed. It's not unusual to order a second test that can corroborate the findings of the first. By the time the results of the second test were issued on May 23rd, there was no doubt that Jane Doe had been telling the truth.

By the end of the meeting, in which Sorrentino clarified what her written documentation was intended to mean, those in the room shook hands and the meeting was adjourned. Thereafter, Commissioner Bratton held a second press conference with reporters, saying on the record that the forensic evidence confirmed the veracity of Jane Doe's claim she was sexually assaulted on April 26, 1994. It was not a hoax.[5] McAlary's headline, "Rape hoax the real crime," had been wrong.

This conclusion to the meeting and subsequent press conference marks a significant turning point in the case. Bratton's public statement confirming the assault represents a reversal of the earlier narrative that had been propagated through McAlary's columns. This public acknowledgment of the truth of Jane Doe's claim was vital in correcting the record and potentially mitigating some of the harm caused by McAlary's columns.

Chapter 5

WHO'S YOUR SOURCE?

> He called me after the first column, you know, kind of saying, "Can you lock this thing down?[1] Can you bail me out? Can you this? Can you that?" I'm like, "Mike, what the fuck is the matter with you?" . . . So where do you jump to this conclusion that a) it's a hoax or b) more outrageously, that she's about to be *arrested*? Excuse me: They didn't arrest *Tawana Brawley*. You think they're gonna lock up some woman in Prospect Park? I don't think so. I mean, I think he's made some giant leaps here. I think he's brought himself way out onto the end of a limb, and I think there's been, you know, a fairly regular attempt . . . to drag the police department out on that limb with him, and we ain't going.[2]

Those were Deputy Commissioner of Public Information John Miller's ridiculing words being recorded on tape, unbeknownst to Miller, by then New York *Newsday* op-ed columnist Gabriel Rotello.[3] This surreptitious recording of Miller's candid remarks provides a rare glimpse into the behind-the-scenes dynamics between law enforcement officials and journalists during a high-profile controversy. The fact that Miller was unaware he was being recorded suggests he felt comfortable speaking freely, potentially revealing more than he would have in an official capacity. This unguarded moment captures the raw frustration and disbelief John Miller apparently felt toward McAlary's columns on Jane Doe's rape case, perhaps because Miller had never intended for McAlary to use what was disclosed as material for his column.

With Miller feeling against the ropes by suspicions he was the unidentified police source feeding misinformation to McAlary, Miller seemed ready to box his way out. Miller may have resented being thrust into the uncomfortable position of needing to defend himself against accusations of complicity in spreading misinformation. Following the pickle McAlary found himself in after being accused of getting the facts wrong in his extraordinary claim that "a lesbian lied about being raped for political purposes," Miller's mocking reenactment of McAlary's alleged plea for help paints a picture of a journalist desperately seeking support from his source after making controversial and unfounded claims.[4] Miller's mocking tone exhibits zero sympathy for the newsman and Miller's desire to distance himself from McAlary.

Perhaps following this hasty, unguarded moment of candidly insulting McAlary, Miller thought better of it as he later publicly denied what he'd told Rotello, though the recorded conversation would be damning and prove otherwise. Miller's attempt to backtrack on his recorded statements in what is considered off-the-record conversations illustrates the fragile balance public officials must maintain with members of the press when discussing high-profile cases and those involved. What was on the tape was exactly what Rotello reported. Before knowing this fact, Miller said to a room full of reporters, "I actually didn't say any of those things to him [Rotello]. I don't know where he got that or how he extrapolated it from the conversation I had with him."[5]

Miller's public denial, made before a group of reporters, represents a bold attempt to discredit Rotello's reporting. This denial, in light of the existence of the recording, raises serious questions about Miller's professional integrity and the extent to which public officials might go to protect themselves or their colleagues in cases that have garnered notoriety. The recording would serve as proof Miller was not misquoted and Miller would have to eat his words and extend an apology to Rotello for putting his journalistic credibility on the line.

In an attempt to save face as well, Mike McAlary denied ever turning to Miller for damage control in the time after his first headline, "Rape hoax the real crime," ran. McAlary's denial that Miller spoke with him contradicts Miller's recorded account, further complicating the narrative surrounding the identity of McAlary's source. Instead, McAlary took a different tack and suggested that his police source was Chief of

Detectives Joseph Borrelli, something McAlary also walked back in due time when Borrelli felt miffed by the implication, and replied, "I haven't spoken to Mike McAlary in I don't know how many years. When was the last time you heard of a reporter giving up a source?"

McAlary's attempt to shift the focus to Borrelli suggests an earnest attempt to maintain the appearance of having high-level connections within the police department from whom he was conceivably receiving reliable information. With the likely desire to bolster the credibility of his wayward reporting, implying access to top-level sources would be one way to defend or excuse printed errors, or the impact of negative public perception of his three columns covering the case. It's also arguable that perhaps McAlary felt naming Borrelli instead of Miller would be one way to shield and deflect any additional attention that might ensnare Miller in further controversy. McAlary would later retract this claim when, under a court-ordered deposition, he disclosed his actual source.

In Commissioner Bratton's first press conference on April 29, 1994, three days after Jane Doe reported to police she was sexually assaulted in Prospect Park, he apologized publicly, saying, "It's unfortunate that apparently, a member of this department shared some thoughts with others that were reported in the media." This public acknowledgment and apology from the commissioner highlighted the seriousness of the situation and the potential damage caused by the unauthorized sharing of information. Bratton's savvy choice of words, saying "thoughts" rather than "facts" or "evidence," deftly downplays the nature of the leaked information, minimizing the perceived impact of the leak while still acknowledging that something inappropriate had occurred. Bratton clearly implied distinction between official police statements and the personal speculations of its individual officers likely went a long way in mitigating a public backlash or damage to the department's credibility. The timing of this press conference, just days after the reported assault and the rapid escalation of the case following the subsequent media controversy, underscored the pressure on the NYPD to respond.

He said that an internal investigation to be led by Chief Borrelli was underway to try and determine who, in his department, was responsible for the leak. Bratton was careful with his comments, nimbly steering clear of the word "misinformation," a strategic approach that managed the situation without explicitly admitting to the dissemination of false information.

He conceded that haste was a factor that compromised the investigative process and resulted in unverified conclusions, offering a partial explanation for missteps. The announcement of an internal investigation led by a high-ranking official like Chief Borrelli signaled the department's commitment to addressing the leak seriously.

He went on to advise, "We don't know who leaked the information, whether it was the investigating officers or somebody who might have information, so don't speculate as to where the leak came from,"[6] perhaps as a way to deflate some of the hype around the high-profile case. His attempt to quell speculation about the source of the leak, potentially protected individuals within the department from premature accusations. Urging others not to speculate, Bratton was likely trying to maintain control over the narrative and prevent further unauthorized disclosures or rumors from circulating. His efforts reflect the delicate balance the commissioner had to strike between addressing the issue transparently and protecting the integrity of both the ongoing criminal investigation and the internal inquiry into the leak. A leak was considered highly irresponsible, because of its potential to not only thwart an ongoing investigation but also to crank up the generalized anxiety of a densely populated metropolitan borough like Brooklyn where new fear and insecurity among residents would find a place to breed.

But rather than reprimand the source, once identified, former New York *Newsday* columnist Gabriel Rotello seemed to suggest in a *Huffington Post* article published years later, in 2013, that Bratton moved to protect the identity of the source instead. The choice to protect rather than reprimand the source could have been viewed, by some, as prioritizing internal relationships over the integrity of the public trust, even if it was within the police commissioner's purview to make such a call. Commissioner Bratton thereby used the power of his position to ensure McAlary's source was never publicly disclosed, even as speculation seemed to tacitly implicate John Miller, "Bratton's boy-wonder spokesman."[7] Without an official acknowledgment that John Miller was the source, unanswered questions surrounding the case persisted.

To provide some context, the commissioner was instrumental in Miller being hired as deputy commissioner for public information, as it was at Bratton's behest, during his first run as commissioner of the NYPD, following Bratton's appointment by then mayor Rudy Giuliani. This appointment marked the beginning of a long and intertwined professional relationship between Bratton and Miller, showcasing Bratton's trust in Miller's capabilities despite Miller's background hailing from the world of journalism rather than law enforcement. The decision to bring a media professional into a high-ranking police department position was unconventional at the time, reflecting Bratton's innovative approach to public relations and information management within the NYPD.

John Miller would go on to have an illustrious career as both a spokesman for law enforcement organizations and agencies as well as a remarkable career as a Peabody and Emmy-award winning investigative reporter and senior correspondent for television networks including ABC News, CBS News, and CNN. His success in both law enforcement and journalism demonstrates his unique ability to bridge these two worlds, leveraging his understanding of media dynamics to enhance communication strategies for law enforcement agencies while also bringing insider knowledge to his reporting on crime and security issues.

In 2003, Miller would report to Bratton a second time, as chief for the Counterterrorism and Criminal Intelligence Bureau, this time on the West Coast with both officials working for the Los Angeles Police Department, in the time after William J. Bratton was appointed chief of police for the LAPD in October of 2002. This move further solidified the professional bond between Bratton and Miller, showcasing their continued collaboration across different law enforcement agencies and geographical locations.

Miller's appointment to a counterterrorism role in Los Angeles also marked a significant shift in his career focus, moving from public information to more specialized security and intelligence work. Notably, Bratton would serve three consecutive five-year terms for the city of Los Angeles before his return to New York. Bratton's extended tenure in Los Angeles provided a stable environment for implementing long-term strategies and reforms, with Miller playing a key role in the department's counterterrorism efforts during this period. This experience in Los Angeles likely contributed to both Bratton's and Miller's expertise in urban policing and security, which they would later bring back to New York City.

The career trajectory of both leaders, whom Bratton identified as a friend of more than twenty years, would align a third time in 2014, just as William Bratton was being sworn in for a second term as NYPD police commissioner on January 2nd of 2014. This third collaboration underscores the depth of their professional relationship and mutual trust, spanning multiple decades and major cities. The timing of their reunification in New York City coincided with evolving challenges in urban policing and counterterrorism, allowing them to apply their combined experiences from Los Angeles to the unique context of New York. John Miller's time in office as deputy commissioner of Intelligence & Counterterrorism for the New York City Police Department began on January 1, 2014, despite the "head-scratching decision to put a former television reporter in such a critical position," according to one high-ranking counterterrorism official who expressed doubt in Bratton's choice.[8]

This skepticism highlights the unconventional nature of Miller's appointment, particularly given the specialized nature of intelligence and counterterrorism work. The doubt expressed by some officials underscores the challenges Miller faced in establishing credibility in this role. The appointment of a former journalist to such a sensitive position within law enforcement was indeed unprecedented, raising questions about the potential implications for the department's operations. By his retirement from the NYPD in June of 2022, Miller would have served under four New York police commissioners,[9] demonstrating his ability to adapt to changing leadership and maintain his position through multiple administrations. This longevity in such a critical role suggests that, despite initial doubts, Miller was able to effectively leverage his unique background and skills to contribute significantly to the NYPD's intelligence and counterterrorism efforts over nearly a decade.

It's amusing to think that when I left Special Victims and considered applying to the Joint Terrorism Task Force, I had a gnawing concern about being rejected because of my involvement in Jane Doe's investigation, especially since it was John Miller who was the head of the JTTF at the time. The irony of potentially being rejected from a professional position due to involvement in a high-profile case that Miller himself had a controversial connection to was not lost on me.

A scene in playwright Nora Ephron's Broadway play *Lucky Guy*,[10] which premiered in 2013, posthumously chronicles Mike McAlary's career, namely his quick ascent from general assignment reporter to becoming a well-known columnist for New York City's most widely read tabloid newspapers. The play, which opened to critical acclaim and starred Tom Hanks in his Broadway debut as McAlary, offers a dramatized portrayal of the journalist's life and career, including the controversial aspects of his reporting. The play seems to imply that it may have been former chief of department John Timoney who was McAlary's unnamed source, though there's no public record attesting to what's implied, nor is there a public denial by the former chief, making it unlikely that we will ever know for sure.

This ambiguity surrounding McAlary's source for the Jane Doe rape case continued to shroud the already contentious story in layers of complexity, highlighting the often murky nature of journalistic sources and the potential consequences of relying on unnamed officials for sensitive information. The play's suggestion regarding Timoney remains speculative to the general public and left audiences to ponder the true identity of McAlary's source and the motivations or carelessness behind a leak that led to such a damaging series of articles.

While McAlary intimates he was conferring with more than one unidentified police source while writing the published news copy of his columns, under a court-ordered deposition in the time after Jane Doe sued the *Daily News* for libel, McAlary said, "John Miller gave me the story." And with that, the prior notion of the existence of more than one unnamed and protected source evaporated into thin air. Miller's use of profanity and informal speech with *Newsday* columnist Gabriel Rotello suggests he was comfortable, and carelessly loose-lipped, speaking candidly about sensitive matters with journalists. The cavalier delivery may have been a characteristic of his conversations with McAlary as well when Miller shared speculative information about Jane Doe's assault without considering the potential consequences.

The supposition that Timoney was in cahoots with Miller was negated, though police spokesman Timothy Trainor, who was deputy chief of the deputy commissioner of public information service, believed otherwise at the time.[11] The disagreement between high-ranking officials suggests that even within law enforcement circles, there was confusion or misinformation about the leak's origin. McAlary may have felt it would give credence to the outrageously sensational claims he was making if there were two Johns instead of one.

This speculation about McAlary's motives points to the potential manipulation of source attribution for journalistic gain. By implying multiple high-level sources, McAlary could have been attempting to add credibility to his controversial reporting, even if this implication was not entirely accurate. An admission that McAlary wasn't above fabricating sources if it served his career and advanced his professional standing, reflects poorly on his journalistic ethics and his mindset at the time.

New York's Shield law, enacted in 1970 and amended thereafter, is a statute that grants broad protections to members of the press, and all persons professionally engaged in a journalistic capacity, to receive absolute protection in shielding the identities of their confidential sources, and qualified protection for others. The law's broad scope allows for the sharing of sensitive information without sources fearing retribution should their identities be revealed. By providing this protection, the law aims to encourage whistleblowers and other sources to come forward with important information, contributing to a more informed public, and a robust free press.

There are some exceptions. As no federal shield law exists, for cases that land in federal court, members of the press may be compelled to give up their sources if it's deemed necessary. In defamation cases, and libel suits, having the source's identity is often very important to being able to prove, often through circumstantial evidence, that the legal standard for actual malice was committed by the journalist, who acted in reckless disregard of the truth. This higher standard of proof was designed to protect speech and freedom of the press, raising the bar for what a plaintiff would need to demonstrate to win a libel or defamation suit.

In the four years before his first column "Rape hoax the real crime" was published on April 28, 1994, McAlary's byline as a columnist appeared on two of New York's major tabloids the *New York Post* and the *New York Daily News*. A reflection of the competitive environment of New York City tabloid journalism in the early 1990s, when McAlary was disgruntled at one paper, or when a lucrative opportunity presented itself, he would cross the street and go to work for the competitor. This willingness to go back and forth between the two tabloids, shows

McAlary's opportunistic approach to building his career, prioritizing personal gain and prominence over loyalty to any particular publication.

When the *Post* sued him for breach of contract in March of 1994, McAlary's sworn testimony revealed with chilling insight his gunslinging approach to executing his daily work. "It was part of his technique, he explained, to make up anecdotes and fabricate quotes to 'illustrate' a story."[12] This admission under oath is troubling, as it directly contradicts fundamental principles of journalistic integrity and ethics. McAlary's cavalier attitude toward factual accuracy raises questions about the reliability of his reporting and reveals the harm caused by his fabrications.

In an affidavit related to the legal actions McAlary was contending with during these years in the early 1990s, author and attorney Martin Garbus writes summarily in his 1998 book *Tough Talk*:

> In a sworn affidavit in that case, McAlary justified a reporter's fabricating events as simply a "writing device." Asked by an attorney to explain "the difference between a writing device and perjury," McAlary replied, under oath, "I don't know the difference 'cause I don't know what the word perjury means."[13]

This irrefutably illustrates McAlary's disregard for the truth and his willingness to manipulate facts for the sake of a compelling story. His professed ignorance of the term "perjury" while under oath is alarming and imbued with a sneer of subterfuge, suggesting either a genuine lack of understanding of ethical boundaries or a deliberate attempt to flip the bird and avoid accountability for his actions.

Garbus seems to suggest that this flagrantly callous exhibition of verbal swagger was part and parcel of a carefully engineered public persona that Mike McAlary would not break from, even under oath. McAlary's brash and unapologetic attitude was not just a personal trait but a calculated professional strategy. By maintaining this persona consistently, even through legal proceedings, McAlary may have wanted to steep in his image as a battle-hardened veteran, regardless of the ethical implications.

Years of conditioning in the rough and tumble world of the tabloid newspaper business, where "getting the story first is more important than getting it right"[14] had permeated into the DNA of his essential character. This mindset highlights the systemic issues within tabloid journalism that may have shaped McAlary's approach to reporting. The emphasis on speed and sensationalism over accuracy reflects a broader problem in media culture, particularly in competitive markets like New York City.

The fierce competition between tabloids and the pressure to produce attention-grabbing content that can boost sales, such as high-profile cases of crime, reinforces a culture that prioritizes speed over the time it would take to verify the facts in every story. This environment creates a breeding ground for journalistic malpractice, where the pursuit of headlines and sales figures can overshadow the fundamental responsibility of reporters to provide accurate, truthful information to the public. This relentless demand for sensational stories and the race to be the first to break news is likely a chronic temptation tempting tabloid journalists to cut corners and to rely too heavily on unverified sources. In McAlary's case, this culture seems to have fostered his cavalier attitude toward factual accuracy and ethical reporting standards, ultimately contributing to the controversial and damaging coverage of the Prospect Park rape case. The consequences of this corrosive informational culture extend beyond individual cases, eroding public trust in the ideological behemoths of media institutions and the criminal justice system, tugging at the fibers that make up the fabric of our tightly woven notions of an informed and just society.

Jill Abramson, the esteemed former Executive Director of the *New York Times*, professes that journalists' reliance on anonymous sources is a part of the media landscape but underscores that "information has so much more credibility when it is attached to a named source."[15] While acknowledging their necessity in certain situations, Abramson's emphasis on the greater credibility of named sources points to the potential pitfalls of relying too heavily on unnamed informants. The use of anonymous sources remains an ongoing debate within the profession. When a source goes unnamed, as the police source did in McAlary's columns, readers are left banking on the credibility of the journalist and the implicit expectation that he would not knowingly violate the public trust.

Unfortunately, when fabrications presented as journalistic work are a "writing device," ascertaining the truth becomes very murky. This reference to McAlary's own admission about fabricating details blurs the line between fact and fiction in journalism, undermining the public's trust and faith in the media as a whole. McAlary's admission to inventing stories and fabricating quotes raises questions about the extent of this practice in his work and whether it was isolated to specific instances, such as his reporting on Jane Doe's rape or a more pervasive issue that cast doubt on his entire body of work as well. Two-time Pulitzer Prize winner and former columnist of the *New York Times* Anthony Lewis commented that McAlary's use of "unnamed sources"[16] was a "blot on our profession."

Using unnamed sources calls into question issues of accountability as it is harder for others to verify information independently, especially when such information has the potential to shape, for instance, policy decisions or other important aspects of our culture. In cases like the Prospect Park rape, where McAlary's reporting had real-world consequences for Jane Doe and the public perception of sexual assault cases, the reliance on an anonymous source becomes a point of contention. The thin line between protecting sources and maintaining transparency in one's reporting continues to be a central issue facing journalists today. When readers and journalistic peers cannot verify the credibility of one's sources, they have the implicit right to question the impartiality of the reporting.

While Mike McAlary was not the first to break the Abner Louima story of the horrendous police brutality, and sodomization of a Haitian immigrant, which drew a spotlight on the need for police reform in light of such inexcusable misconduct, McAlary was the first to interview Louima by his hospital bedside. This exclusive interview demonstrated McAlary's tenacity as a journalist and the story exposed deep-rooted issues within the NYPD, and sparked widespread outrage and calls for systemic change.

For the columns he wrote on Louima, which McAlary called "a story to stop the city,"[17] he was awarded the Pulitzer Prize for Commentary in April of 1998. Despite the Prospect Park rape case which stood out as a major ethical lapse that tarnished his reputation, caused real harm to Jane Doe, and represented an indelible stain on his overall record, his coverage of police brutality cemented his reputation as a formidable journalist capable of tackling complex and controversial subjects. McAlary seemed to naturally intuit how the Louima story had the potential to reshape public discourse on police conduct and racial justice.

An illustration of his inexhaustible work ethic, and perhaps indicative of the ultra-competitive nature of tabloid journalism in New York City, where getting the scoop could make or break a reporter's career, McAlary, who had been battling advanced colon cancer following a diagnosis in 1997, abandoned a chemotherapy session mid-drip in order to get an exclusive with Louima. This resulted in the first of his nine columns, published on August 13, 1997. Despite past blunders, his dedication to his craft exemplified McAlary's commitment to bringing important stories to light. McAlary succumbed to his illness on Christmas Day, 1998, at the age of forty-one, his untimely death coming just months after receiving the Pulitzer Prize.

Rape hoax the real crime

Photo 1 Mike McAlary, "Rape hoax the real crime," *New York Daily News*, April 28, 1994. *Source*: From kellyannemayberry [User], Newspapers.com, February 5, 2020.

No easy task exposing a lie

IN THE BEGINNING, there was Tawana Brawley and the rape that never happened.

The question, then and now, is how do you prove a lie? How can the cops in Brooklyn, for example, prove that this week's hoaxer wasn't raped the other night in Prospect Park? They know she lied, but they're letting her fade away, worried that genuine victims might not come forward.

Brawley, of course, did not fade away. Without a shred of evidence, her lawyers accused innocent people. The howls of racial injustice became so loud and incredible that the governor intervened and gave the case to a state prosecutor named John Ryan.

This time the rape allegations and the race card are playing in Queens. For a month or so now, two lawyers have claimed that a cop sodomized at least five livery drivers. The accusations are wild. Again, they are being reported, no questions asked, in certain newspapers. Radio carries live reports on the so-called Rockaway Five.

Now, if there is a cop sodomizing men out in Queens, it is a deeply disturbing story. But another fiction against cops is equally scary.

Again, John Ryan will determine the truth. The man who proved the Brawley outrage a lie now heads the criminal investigation unit in Queens.

The same people who paraded outside the Brawley grand jury with signs reading, "The white man is the devil," are now on parade outside the Queens courthouse. Ryan is not intimidated by angry shouts. He was crushed a couple of years ago when white students accused of sexually assaulting a black woman at St. Johns bragged, "We'll just make her into another Tawana." The same district attorney who doggedly pressed the prosecution of that case, Richard Brown, is now being accused of bigotry.

Ryan has found no evidence of a crime in the livery cab case, but he is still searching.

At this point, he is not saying anything. He wants to be sure, if he

See McALARY Page 20

Photo 2 Mike McAlary, "No easy task exposing a lie," ***New York Daily News,*** **April 29, 1994.** ***Source*****: Copyright © 1994 New York Daily News. All rights reserved. Distributed by Tribune Content Agency, LLC. Reprinted with permission.**

I'm right, but that's no reason to cheer

ONE MORNING you open the newspapers, and suddenly *you* are the story. There is a front-page article in The New York Times questioning your credibility. People are calling you a liar.

Some reporters have accused you of being rash, impolite or worse. You rushed to judgment, they say. There are, unfortunately, too many days when these observations are true. You *are* quick to judge. But when the column-writing business is going right, you are even faster, hopefully, to the truth.

On this day you wrote about the woman you said cried wolf in Prospect Park. There was no evidence, police investigators assured you, to support the alleged victim's claim of rape in a public place. Some even said the alleged rape smelled like a hoax. The alleged victim, they said, had asked to read a statement about rape at a gay rally. The cops saw this as motive to lie. You thought it might be a good idea to arrest people who reported rape to gain publicity. Maybe you were wrong about that.

By afternoon the agenda people were screaming. Police Commissioner William Bratton was worried about his department's reputation. He did not like the idea of scaring off real rape victims. Bratton was right to be worried for his Police Department. So he apologized for any police role in questioning the woman's truthfulness. But he was careful, incidentally, not to comment on the alleged victim's truthfulness.

That night, police began to circulate reports of a lab test. Semen was found, a police spokesman reported, on the woman's shorts and vagina. It would be very hard to find semen in a rape hoax, reporters reasoned. This newspaper, and others, backed away the next day.

In the morning I telephoned a couple of law enforcement sources with knowledge of the woman's case and mentioned the semen discovery. I offered to apologize to the woman. Apology, by the way, is generally a good thing in this business. When you are wrong, it is a good idea to admit the mistake fast. People will then say, "He's the first person to admit it when he is wrong."

Oddly, apologies add to your credibility.

But on this occasion, one of the sources said, "Stand your ground. The lab is wrong."

An hour later details of the lab mistake became more obvious. No semen had been found. At best, the lab reported, the substance was saliva, male or female. The editors stood behind your story. It took some grace and bravery, but they would not apologize for being right.

The papers came out the next day, and the same reporters who accused you of being too quick to judge, all wrote that semen had been found. "Police find evidence of rape," shouted the headlines.

Police investigators asked you to sit on the story. There weren't any physical bruises or scratches. No witnesses have been found. There was no evidence, then or now, to support the woman's rape claim. She didn't get a good look at the guy, and yet made a detailed sketch. The alleged rapist's coat was never found. Neither were the alleged victim's groceries.

In fact, when the police stopped a black man fitting the description given by the alleged victim, she called the cops racist. She delivered her statement, as promised, to the rally. The alleged victim got more publicity than she dreamed about.

She was issuing press releases by the weekend. The alleged victim was questioning police for questioning her story. Semen was found, she said. The police knew that and still questioned me because I am a lesbian, she insisted.

And still you remained quiet.

Maybe, if you gave her room, the police theorized, the alleged victim would back

See **McALARY** Page 30

Photo 3 Mike McAlary, "I'm right but that's no reason to cheer," ***New York Daily News*****, May 13, 1994.** *Source*: **Copyright © 1994 New York Daily News. All rights reserved. Distributed by Tribune Content Agency, LLC. Reprinted with permission.**

Enough crime without inventing it

ONCE IN BOSTON, a young white man told a story about a shooting. Charles Stuart falsely claimed his wife had been shot by a black man. Also wounded, he made a frantic call from his cellular phone. In that town, remember, the cops went out and arrested a black suspect who then confessed. Stuart's fiction became a racial parable for our times.

In Brooklyn, you fear today, someone has tried to ruin part of this city with the same lie. A woman said she was walking through Prospect Park with two bags of groceries Tuesday afternoon when, she said, a black man dragged her up a hill and raped her. But unlike the Boston cops, these police are more skeptical. In fact, they believe they are being lied to.

It is an outrageous story, really. The woman, who is black and 27 years old, describes herself as a social activist. All we really know about her is that she has an active imagination. She is supposed to appear at a gay and lesbian rally this weekend to protest crime. She promised yesterday to deliver a first-person speech on her own rape.

But last night everyone who heard the woman's story about the alleged rape was calling it a hoax. The woman, who probably will wind up being arrested herself, invented the crime, they said, to promote her rally. Even in New York, this is a strange motive. The terrible thing is that you don't have to invent terrible crimes in New York. A false report of rape by a woman looking for publicity is a crime against all women. It diminishes all rape victims.

Immediately after the Prospect Heights woman flagged down a patrol car, she gave them a description. Black man, she said. The description was her invention. (Yesterday, she even helped police draw a composite sketch.) So the cops started driving around the park looking for a black man with a leather coat. The cops stopped one black man and started to question him. The woman, they said, became agitated.

"Why are you stopping him?" the alleged victim protested. "Just because he is black?"

The cops were amazed and appalled. After all, they later told superiors, they stopped the guy only because he fit *her* description. And then, they noticed the woman had no marks on her to support her tale of being dragged by the neck up a hill. They began to get nervous.

Fear was beginning to spread in Brooklyn by the 11 o'clock news. Prospect Park was a crime scene again. Rapists were back this spring with the leaves. Last year, one woman was raped in the park. Another woman was grabbed. A teacher named Winslow on a bike was shot and killed. All these crimes were real and scary. They stopped the city. And then you have this woman coming forward with her fiction five years after the jogger in Central Park. TV is running tape of the laughing Coney Island rapists. I wonder what those real victims and survivors will think of the hoaxer's speech on violence.

The woman said she was dragged up Lookout Hill. The cops found no drag marks or groceries. And she said there were witnesses. But cops could not find them.

Someone was saying last night that the woman had no injuries or bruises consistent with a rape, or even traces of semen. When a special victim's squad detective tried to see if there were scratches on her back, the woman caught on fast.

"He took off his coat and laid it on the ground," the woman now insisted. "He put me on top of the coat."

Chivalry at a rape scene. Great, now the cops were looking for Sir Walter Raleigh-turned-rapist. The cops did not find a jacket.

The women was kind of vocal about being a lesbian. This wouldn't mean anything, incidentally, if a rape occurred. The cops are afraid the woman will try and claim today or tomorrow that police are not taking her seriously because of her sexual preference. Hey, it will make a good speech at the rally. But who is to say that some of the cops investigating this case aren't gay and lesbian? Not all cops are straight, any more than all blacks are rapists. But the hoaxer will stick to the script she invented.

THIS IS ALL so stupid, really. Scaring a whole city won't help anyone's cause. In Brooklyn, you have the woman who cried wolf. A lot of cops were in Prospect Park on Tuesday night, after the rape was reported. They wanted ... catch a rapist. They were spread out pretty good, looking.

Several hours later a real victim reported he had been mugged at the park. Blood marked the real crime scene. The cops rushed in to help. Two of their cars crashed in their haste to be noble. One of them died in the car crash. He was taken to the same hospital — Methodist — as the alleged rape victim. The cop died and the woman lived on, to lie again. They will have his funeral this weekend. It is all the rally you will ever need on crime.

...gan to get nervous.
Fear was beginning to spread in Brooklyn by the 11 o'clock news. Prospect Park was a crime scene again. Rapists were back this spring with the leaves. Last year, one woman was raped in the park. Another woman was grabbed. A teacher named Winslow on a bike was shot and killed. All these crimes were real and scary. They stopped the city. And then you have this woman coming forward with her fiction five years after the jogger in Central Park. TV is running tape of the laughing Coney Island rapists. I wonder what those real victims and survivors will think of the hoaxer's speech on violence.
The woman said she was dragged up Lookout Hill. The cops found no drag marks or groceries. And she said there were witnesses. But cops could not find them.
Someone was saying last night that the woman had no
...ght, any more than all blacks are rapists. But the hoaxer will stick to the script she invented.
THIS IS ALL so stupid, really. Scaring a whole city won't help anyone's cause. In Brooklyn, you have the woman who cried wolf. A lot of cops were in Prospect Park on Tuesday night, after the rape was reported. They wanted ... catch a rapist. They were spread out pretty good, looking.
Several hours later a real victim reported he had been mugged at the park. Blood marked the real crime scene. The cops rushed in to help. Two of their cars crashed in their haste to be noble. One of them died in the car crash. He was taken to the same hospital — Methodist — as the alleged rape victim. The cop died and the woman lived on, to lie again. They will have his funeral this weekend. It is all the rally you will ever need on crime.

—

Photo 4 Mike McAlary, "Enough crime without inventing it," *New York Daily News*, ca. May 1994. *Source*:

Chapter 6

A HIGHER STANDARD OF PROOF

> The police had substantiated my story, the lab reports proved I had been raped, and every paper in the city was reporting the case accurately. I had put the early columns behind me. I believed that at that point even McAlary understood he had wronged me and was ready to let it go. When the last column appeared, days after police confirmed the attack on me, I knew I had to do something.[1]
>
> —Jane Doe, plaintiff in *Doe v. Daily News*, L.P.

Jane Doe sought the help of Attorney Martin Garbus, an expert on the First Amendment, who, over a long and notable career defending free speech in the United States and around the world, is recognized as one of the best trial lawyers in the country. Garbus's reputation as a First Amendment expert and his extensive experience in high-profile cases made him a formidable choice for Jane Doe's legal representation. His work on landmark cases involving civil rights, freedom of speech, and press freedom had established him as a leading figure in constitutional law.

Garbus served as co-counsel in *Ashton v. Kentucky*, a landmark Supreme Court decision in 1966 that effectively ended criminal libel laws in the United States. The case involved Steve Ashton, who had been convicted of criminal libel for circulating a pamphlet criticizing local officials during a labor dispute in Kentucky. The Supreme Court unanimously reversed the conviction, ruling that the criminal libel statute did not withstand constitutional scrutiny under the First Amendment. This landmark decision was significant because it struck down laws that had allowed prosecutors to bring criminal charges against individuals for publishing false and malicious statements. The ruling greatly expanded free speech protections and freedom of the press in the United States and demonstrated Attorney Garbus's dedicated commitment to defending civil liberties and challenging unjust laws.

Upon meeting Jane Doe, Garbus found her to be highly credible and an accurate historian of her April 1994 rape in Prospect Park, as well as the cascade of events that followed when her story was unwittingly splashed across tabloid headlines. This initial impression of Jane Doe's credibility was crucial, as it formed the foundation for Garbus's commitment to her case and his belief in the importance of challenging the false narrative that had been propagated in the media.

Garbus writes, in his book *Tough Talk*, "more than thirty years of practice had left me with a finely honed sense of a witness's devotion to the truth. I believed Jane Doe was telling me the truth, and that her account of the events was as accurate as she could make it."[2] His decades of experience in evaluating witnesses and their testimonies lent considerable weight to his belief in Jane Doe's account in the face of public skepticism and media scrutiny. Garbus's conviction of Jane Doe's truthfulness not only informed his legal strategy but also served as a powerful counterpoint to the doubts cast upon her story by McAlary's columns. This unwavering belief in his client's veracity was particularly significant given the high-profile nature of the case and the challenges posed by McAlary's status as a prominent journalist. Garbus's stance demonstrated his willingness to challenge established narratives and confront powerful media figures in pursuit of justice for his client.

Weighing his sense of moral obligation to practice the law in service of doing the right thing, Garbus accepted Jane Doe as his client despite the hailstorm of criticism that he'd be forced to ride out. This decision could not have been made lightly and demonstrated Garbus's commitment to justice and his willingness to take on challenging cases, even when they went against the grain of conventional legal practice.

He knew representing a plaintiff in a libel suit, where the co-defendants were a well-known columnist and a notable news organization, would be highly unpopular and poorly received by his community of legal peers who almost exclusively beheld a staunch code of conduct to never, under any circumstances, undermine the freedom of the press. This unwritten rule among legal professionals highlighted the potential professional risks Garbus was taking by accepting Jane Doe's case.

Doing so would be tantamount to a betrayal, with significant negative repercussions to Attorney Garbus's professional career a near certainty, placing him in a precarious position and alienating him from his colleagues. The potential consequences of his decision underscored the gravity of Garbus's choice and the strength of his conviction in Jane Doe's case. Believing that Jane Doe's civil case had merit, Garbus was willing to stake his reputation as a First Amendment attorney by siding with the plaintiff and daring to hold a popular tabloid newspaper accountable. This bold move demonstrated Garbus's dedication to pursuing justice, even when it meant challenging powerful institutions and risking his own professional standing. His willingness to take on this civil case, despite the potential backlash, showcased his commitment to upholding the rights of individuals who had been wronged, regardless of the opposing party's influence or status in the media world. By accepting Jane Doe as a client, Garbus was not only advocating for her personal justice but also challenging the broader notion that the press should be immune from accountability in cases of potentially harmful reporting.

In June of 1994, Garbus filed the libel suit seeking $12M for his client in both compensatory and punitive damages. This substantial sum reflected the perceived severity of the harm done to Jane Doe by McAlary's columns and the newspaper's publication of them. The high-profile nature of the case and the significant damages sought underscored the seriousness with which Garbus and his client viewed the alleged libel.

By February 1997, the judge presiding over the case granted the defense's motion for summary judgment and ruled to dismiss the case without proceeding to a trial, stating that the defendants had "absolute privilege to comment on matters of public concern," a decisive affirmation of First Amendment protections for the press. This ruling highlighted the strong legal protections afforded to journalists and media organizations in the United States, particularly when reporting on issues deemed to be of public interest.

The judge's decision to dismiss the case without a trial was a significant setback for Jane Doe and Garbus, effectively ending their legal challenge before they could present their full case to a jury. The ruling's emphasis on "absolute privilege" for the press in matters of public concern demonstrated broad legal protections for speech and the high bar set for plaintiffs in libel cases against media entities, especially when the subject matter is considered newsworthy. These First Amendment protections are rooted in the belief that robust public debate on important issues is essential to a functioning democracy, even if that debate sometimes includes statements that are factually inaccurate. This ruling was consistent with the judiciary's reluctance to impose penalties on journalists for their reporting, even in cases where the accuracy of that reporting is disputed. However, it left questions about the recourse available to plaintiffs like Jane Doe who believe they have been wronged by media coverage unresolved.

A disappointing outcome for his client, Garbus predicted if it had gone to trial, "a jury weighing [McAlary's] credibility against Jane Doe's would not hesitate to come down on the side of the plaintiff."[3] This statement from Garbus reflects his confidence in Jane Doe's credibility and the strength of their case, suggesting that he believed a jury would have been more sympathetic to Jane Doe's account than the judge's legal interpretation. Garbus's assertion highlights the potential disconnect between legal rulings based on technical interpretations of the law and the more empathetic judgments that might be rendered by a jury of peers. Garbus's belief that a jury would side with Jane Doe suggests that he felt the emotional impact of her story and the perceived harm caused by McAlary's columns would resonate strongly with ordinary citizens. This perspective emphasizes the human element of the case, which can sometimes be overshadowed by legal technicalities in summary judgments.

Furthermore, Garbus's statement implies a critique of the summary judgment process, which prevented the case from reaching a jury trial. By expressing his confidence in a potential jury verdict, he indirectly questions whether the legal system, in this instance, truly served the interests of justice as he perceived them. This highlights the ongoing debate in legal circles about the appropriate balance between judicial efficiency through summary judgments and the right to have one's case heard by a jury of peers.

Jane Doe's real name was never publicly named by McAlary in his columns, because she was the victim of a sex crime and her identity was therefore protected. This protection of her identity was in line with standard journalistic practices and legal requirements for shielding the identities of sexual assault victims. The anonymity was crucial for her privacy and safety, given how the controversy surrounding McAlary's reporting ratcheted the story's profile to the level of spectacle. In spite of her relative anonymity, New York State Supreme Court Judge Charles E. Ramos adjudicated *Doe. v. Daily News* by designating Jane Doe as a public figure.[4] This designation was a pivotal and controversial aspect of the case, as it significantly impacted the legal standards applied to Jane's libel suit.

An overly broad application of Jane Doe's participation in the gay and lesbian advocacy organizations she chose to affiliate with, acted as the lynchpin by which Judge Ramos interpreted Jane as having crossed the chasm from being a private citizen to becoming a public figure because such engagement was considered "social activism."[5] This interpretation of Jane Doe's activism as sufficient grounds for classifying her as a public figure raised significant questions about the boundaries between private and public life. This classification was controversial because it seemed to contradict the anonymity that had been maintained throughout the media coverage of her case. It raised questions about how someone whose identity was protected could simultaneously be considered a public figure in the eyes of the law. It also raised questions about whether involvement in activism or speaking out about one's experiences should automatically elevate someone to public figure status, potentially discouraging victims from coming forward or engaging in advocacy for fear of losing their legal protections in defamation cases.

Judge Ramos's reasoning came as a surprise to Attorney Martin Garbus, who wrote in his book *Tough Talk* that "had [Jane's actual name] been published, it would have been recognized only by those who already knew her."[6] The apparent contradiction in Jane Doe being deemed a public figure despite the fact that her true identity remained unknown to the general public due to her status as a sexual assault victim stretched the legal definition of "public figures" in defamation cases.

Typically, in a libel suit, in which the plaintiff is recognized as a private citizen, the standard of proof would be to establish that negligence had occurred, in which the defendant had committed a breach of duty in exercising a reasonable level of care to ensure and verify that the information to be published was accurate. This lower standard for private citizens reflects the law's recognition that ordinary individuals should have greater protection against defamatory statements, as they generally do not have the same access to media platforms to counter false claims as public figures do. The negligence standard acknowledges that private individuals are more vulnerable to reputational harm and less equipped to defend themselves in the court of public opinion.

Proving negligence would have been easier than proving actual malice because an act of negligence, such as forgetting to fact-check one's writing, or failing to corroborate information from multiple sources, is objective and generally more straightforward to prove, whereas proving there's evidence of actual malice is a subjective dive into the defendant's intent. This distinction highlights the significant challenge Jane Doe faced in her lawsuit once classified as a public figure as the shift from a negligence standard to an actual malice standard dramatically increased the burden of proof for Jane, creating a substantial hurdle in her pursuit for justice.

The difference between negligence and actual malice is not just in the nature of the proof required but also in the standard of evidence needed. Whereas negligence can be proven by a "preponderance of evidence," actual malice requires "clear and convincing evidence" for civil cases. The "preponderance of evidence" standard means that the plaintiff must show that it is more likely than not that the defendant was negligent. In contrast, "clear and convincing evidence" is a higher standard, requiring that the evidence be substantially more probable to be true than not.

It was the landmark 1964 Supreme Court decision of the *New York Times v. Sullivan* which set the standard of "actual malice." This case fundamentally changed the perspective of defamation law in the United States, as it related to public officials, defined as anyone who had a substantial responsibility in government-related affairs. This definition delineated a specific category of individuals to whom this new, more stringent standard would apply. In order for a public official to win their libel suit, the burden of proof that the defendant had acted with actual malice rested with the plaintiff. This shift in the burden of proof was a significant departure from previous legal standards and represented a strong protection for freedom of speech and press. This high bar was intentionally set to ensure that public debate on important issues would not be stifled by the threat of libel suits. Prior to Sullivan, the plaintiff only needed to prove that a false statement had been made in order for the defendant to be liable. This lower standard had often resulted in self-censorship by the press and others, fearful of the potential legal consequences of criticizing public officials.

Following this important decision, it became much more difficult for public officials to weaponize the legal system to intimidate the press. The Sullivan ruling effectively created a constitutional safeguard for the media and individuals criticizing government officials, ensuring that honest mistakes or minor inaccuracies would not lead to ruinous libel judgments. This protection was seen as essential for maintaining a free press capable of holding those in power accountable. The decision has since been expanded to cover not just public officials but also public figures more broadly, further strengthening the protections for free speech in matters of public concern. The Sullivan standard continues to be a cornerstone of American defamation law, balancing the need to protect individual reputations with the paramount importance of uninhibited public discourse in a democratic society.

It was the *Curtis Publishing Co. v. Butts* decision that followed in 1967, which extended the same standard of actual malice to all public figures in order to win a libel case. The *Curtis Publishing Co. v. Butts* case involved a lawsuit by a former athletic director at the University of Georgia, who was accused of fixing a football game. The court's decision to apply the actual malice standard to this case, despite the plaintiff not being a government official, signaled a recognition that public debate extends beyond just matters of governance. This expansion of the Sullivan standard marked a significant development in defamation law, broadening the protection of free speech beyond criticism of government officials to include a wider range.

The Supreme Court defined public figures as those "who have assumed roles of prominence in the affairs of society," achieving a level of fame, as well as those who have "thrust themselves to the forefront of particular public controversies." This definition created two categories of public figures: all-purpose public figures who are widely known and influential, and limited-purpose public figures who become involved in specific public controversies. The creation of these categories acknowledged that individuals can become part of public discourse in different ways and to varying degrees, necessitating a nuanced approach to applying the actual malice standard.

All-purpose public figures are individuals who have pervasive fame or notoriety across a broad spectrum of issues. These might include celebrities, high-profile business leaders, or nationally recognized politicians. The judiciary has reasoned that such individuals have significant access to media channels to counter false claims and have voluntarily accepted a role in public life that invites scrutiny and commentary. Limited-purpose public figures, on the other hand, are those who have voluntarily injected themselves or been drawn into a particular public controversy. This category might include activists, whistleblowers, or individuals involved in high-profile cases.

Notably, Judge Ramos's decision to classify Jane Doe as a public figure seems to be an overly broad interpretation because rape victims rarely seek public attention in the aftermath of the violence they endured. This classification raises questions about the appropriateness of applying the public figure standard to victims of sexual assault, particularly when they have not voluntarily sought the spotlight. The decision appears to conflate Jane Doe's involvement in advocacy organizations with a deliberate thrust into public controversy, overlooking the sensitive nature of sexual assault cases and the importance of protecting victims' privacy. It asks us, as a culture, where we draw the line between what the public deserves to know, as a matter of interest about Jane Doe and her plight, and protecting vulnerable individuals, such as Jane Doe and other anonymous sexual assault victims, from inaccurate reporting that has the potential to do more harm.

These SCOTUS decisions, which set a precedent in better securing freedom of the press, gave journalists the runway to report candidly without excessive preoccupation over any reprobation their writing might incur when covering stories involving public officials and public figures. This legal protection allowed for more robust and critical reporting, fostering a media environment where journalists could more freely investigate and report on powerful individuals and institutions. The reduced threat of libel suits encouraged a more vigorous press, essential for maintaining an informed citizenry and holding those in power accountable.

More practically, members of the press were greatly alleviated by the fear of going to work one day to find out the publication they worked for was being sued over something they had reported. This reduction in legal risk had significant implications for the day-to-day work of journalists and news organizations. It allowed for quicker publication of important stories without the need for excessive legal vetting, which could delay or even prevent the release of time-sensitive information. The impact of these rulings extended far beyond the courtroom, fundamentally reshaping the landscape of American journalism. The increased legal protection encouraged more investigative journalism, as reporters and editors could pursue controversial or sensitive stories with less fear of legal repercussions. Journalists became more emboldened to ask tough questions, pursue controversial stories, and challenge official narratives. This newfound legal protection fostered a more adversarial relationship between the press and those in power, which many argue is essential for a functioning democracy. It allowed journalists to report on matters of public concern even when they couldn't be absolutely certain of every detail, as long as they weren't acting with reckless disregard for the truth. This standard recognized that some factual errors are inevitable in the fast-paced world of news reporting and that the public interest is better served by a press that is free to report on important issues without paralyzing fear of legal consequences.

However, this freedom also came with the responsibility to maintain high standards of journalistic integrity and accuracy, as the protection did not grant absolute immunity and still required adherence to ethical reporting practices. The "actual malice" standard, while high, was not insurmountable, and public figures could still prevail in libel cases if they could prove that false statements were made with knowledge of their falsity or reckless disregard for the truth. In recent years, there have been debates about whether these protections have gone too far, particularly in the age of social media and "fake news." Some argue that the high bar set by the "actual malice" standard makes it too difficult for public figures to protect their reputations against false or misleading information.

It's easy to see how in more restrictive times, or for journalists living in countries where their voices are hamstrung by oppressive regimes, a reporter would consciously or subconsciously walk back how he or she chooses to deploy their journalistic voice. This self-censorship could manifest in various ways, from softening critical language to avoiding certain topics altogether. The fear of legal repercussions or other forms of retaliation can significantly impact the depth and breadth of reporting. Journalists may have felt compelled or obligated to dilute the force of their arguments, constantly looking over their shoulders, and worried about potential legal consequences, severely undercutting their role as effective watchdogs or moral arbiters. The threat of lawsuits was likely particularly chilling for smaller news organizations or individual journalists who may not have had the financial resources to defend themselves in court, even if their reporting was accurate and in the public interest. This dynamic created an uneven playing field where only well-funded media outlets may have felt secure enough to pursue hard-hitting investigative journalism, leaving many important stories uncovered.

Though Judge Charles E. Ramos had a reputation for being fair and impartial, he may have ruled to dismiss the case swayed by extrinsic factors such as the desire to avoid getting on the wrong side of a prominent and well-circulated newspaper like the *New York Daily News*. This speculation raises questions about the potential influence of media power on judicial decisions, especially in cases involving high-profile news organizations. Potentially negative coverage could have endangered career aspirations, suggesting that judges, despite their commitment to impartiality, might be susceptible to concerns about their public image and future prospects. This points to the broader implications of how public perception and media portrayal can potentially impact the justice system, even indirectly.

To establish evidence for the claim that Mike McAlary was guilty of actual malice and reckless disregard of the truth, Jane Doe's lawyer pointed to McAlary's third column printed on Friday, May 13, 1994, that has him insisting, as the headline read, "I'm right, but that's no reason to cheer," denying the veracity of unequivocal lab findings that were consistent with Jane Doe's claim that she was raped. This column, published after scientific evidence had emerged supporting Jane Doe's account, could be seen as a clear indication of McAlary's unwillingness to acknowledge facts that contradicted his initial reporting.

The lawyer may have emphasized that McAlary's continued insistence on his original narrative, even in the face of contradictory forensic evidence, went beyond mere negligence or error. By doubling down on his "hoax" claim when presented with lab results supporting Jane Doe's account, McAlary's actions could be interpreted as deliberately ignoring or dismissing evidence that didn't fit his preconceived narrative. The headline itself, "I'm right, but that's no reason to cheer," could be seen as further evidence of McAlary's stubborn adherence to his original story, prioritizing his reputation over journalistic integrity. This behavior aligns with the definition of actual malice as established in *New York Times Co. v. Sullivan*, which includes "reckless disregard of whether it was false or not."

In his deposition, "McAlary claimed that the police were telling the media and the public one story—that evidence confirmed the rape and a vigorous investigation was proceeding—while feeding McAlary, and only McAlary, an entirely different story—that a hoax had been perpetrated and no investigation was being pursued."[7] Such a claim, if true, would raise serious questions about the integrity of the police department's communication practices given the significant discrepancy between the official police narrative and the information McAlary claimed to have received privately. McAlary's reliance on a single, unnamed source for such a controversial story could be seen as a failure to meet basic journalistic standards of verification and due diligence, especially when he claimed that the information he received from his source contradicted official statements and forensic evidence.

When McAlary conceded in his testimony that Deputy Commissioner of Public Information John Miller was his only source, he purported that while Miller never used the word "hoax," a term that was featured prominently in the *Daily News* columns, McAlary claimed Miller used variants thereof including "bullshit." While strong language like "bullshit" by a high-ranking police official, if accurate, would indicate a dismissive attitude toward the victim's claims, McAlary's extrapolation of the profane term to the definitive term "hoax" in his published columns shows how the embellishment of word choice resulted in a misrepresentation of sourced information. Taking semantic liberties, without the direct use of a quotation, shows the consequential pitfalls of paraphrasing when choices about terminology have an amplifying effect that impacts both the victim and her investigation.

The defense that McAlary was misled by Miller to publish what he did seems feeble, especially because Miller's testimony refuted much of McAlary's account under oath. This discrepancy between McAlary's claims and Miller's testimony raises significant questions as the contradiction between the two accounts suggests that McAlary knowingly embellished the information he received from Miller. McAlary's reliance on Miller as his sole source for a sensitive story about sexual assault, and his failure to seek additional sources or perspectives before publishing such definitive claims about Jane Doe, could be seen as a breach of journalistic duty.

Despite a second round of depositions, Judge Ramos dismissed the plaintiff's right to seek damages for harm done to her reputation due to McAlary's columns and decided that Jane Doe had insufficient evidence "that the defendant's report and commenting on the events surrounding the assault on her were grossly inaccurate or unreasonable."[8] Judge Ramos's interpretation is subjective as there are no legal standards or thresholds for proving evidence was "grossly inaccurate or unreasonable." His decision to dismiss the plaintiff's right to seek damages, despite the conflicting testimonies and the serious nature of the allegations, highlights the challenge Jane Doe faced in seeking legal recourse.

McAlary's lawyers, including Kenneth A. Caruso, made the argument that, because Mike McAlary is a columnist, "McAlary's statements should be considered opinion, and therefore protected by the First Amendment."[9] The distinction between fact and opinion is crucial in defamation cases, as opinions generally receive stronger constitutional protection. While all members of the press are bound by journalistic standards and editorial oversight, a tabloid columnist is given more range to develop and capitalize on a writing style that may be more provocative, employing hyperbole in an opinionated column, for example, as a tool of written rhetoric, more liberally than straight reporters. This distinction recognizes the different roles and expectations associated with various forms of journalism. Columnists, by nature of their position, are often expected to provide commentary, analysis, and personal perspectives on events, which may involve more subjective interpretations than straight news reporting.

McAlary's hard-hitting, aggressive writing style was part of his personal brand and a way to engage loyal readers, who may have found his combative writing style to be part of his appeal and also a deliberate strategy to build and maintain his readership. It can be argued that McAlary's controversial columns are consistent with his established persona as a provocateur and that sensationalized assertions would have been understood by his readers as part of McAlary's characteristic style rather than as straightforward factual claims.

This perspective aligns with the legal concept of the "reasonable reader" standard, which considers how an average reader would interpret the statements in question. Courts often consider factors such as the context in which the statements appear, the medium of publication, and the author's reputation and brand style when determining whether a statement should be classified as fact or opinion. The line between fact and opinion is not always clear-cut, and courts have grappled with this distinction in numerous cases. The Supreme Court has held that simply labeling a statement as "opinion" does not automatically shield it from defamation claims as some statements, while framed as opinions, can still imply factual assertions that may be subject to defamation laws.

While McAlary may have felt it was within his purview to push the outer boundaries of ethical journalism, no columnist has the impunity to make defamatory statements in the guise of written "opinion." There is a distinction between protected opinion and potentially libelous statements. Even opinions should find their basis in underlying and relevant facts. Columnists have a responsibility to ground their opinions in verifiable information, a reasonable expectation of responsible journalism that respects the boundaries of truth and fairness.

At the very least, McAlary could have responded to the media backlash and public outrage following the publication of "Rape Hoax the real crime," with a greater measure of acknowledgment for how his words may have been harming Jane Doe. For him to have written his columns in a way that showed little to no consideration of the destructive effects that resulted from writing callously about sensitive subject matter dealt in harm rather than mitigating its effects. As a prominent columnist with a wide readership, this lack of foresight on his part to consider or anticipate the potential consequences of his reporting revealed that McAlary had a blind side. The negative consequences extended far beyond his immediate coverage of Jane Doe's case and created a broader inhospitable climate of treating rape victims with skepticism.

Despite what Garbus called a "high-stakes legal proceeding," Judge Charles E. Ramos granted the defense's motion to dismiss on summary judgment which presumed that the defense was entitled to win based on established facts saying, "This court finds that Mr. McAlary was given information by the police that was inaccurate, but that he reported that misinformation accurately and drew reasonable inferences from it."[10] Though there were erroneous details in McAlary's columns, First Amendment protections still applied. Judge Ramos's decision suggests that as long as a journalist accurately reports the information they receive, even if that information later proves to be incorrect, they may be shielded from liability. The key factor in determining liability is not the absolute accuracy of the information he reported, but rather McAlary's faithful representation of the information he received from Miller. The judge's decision prioritizes the broader societal interest of a free and robust press over the potential harm to individuals who may be affected by inaccurate reporting. While the law protects journalists who make good-faith efforts to report accurately based on the information available to them, it may also potentially shield those who are more culpable by degrees of journalistic practice, and less diligent.

Martin Garbus filed an appeal on behalf of his client, but Jane Doe was tired of the protracted legal battle and subsequently, they opted to drop the case. Her fatigue after years of fighting for justice is a common experience for many victims who pursue legal action, often finding the process itself to be emotionally draining and re-traumatizing. This exhaustion can be especially pronounced for victims of sexual assault, whose lives have already been upended by their traumatic experiences.

While Garbus felt there were potential grounds to go after the police department for the damage incurred due to leaked misinformation, Jane Doe had little interest in doing so, due to feeling emotionally spent and fatigued, after years of fighting the good fight. Had she decided to pursue legal action against the NYPD, it would have involved another lengthy and complex legal process, exposing Jane Doe to further scrutiny. Her decision to prioritize her well-being over pursuing further legal action reflects the often overlooked human aspect of such cases, where the pursuit of justice comes at a significant personal cost to the victim.

Chapter 7

REOPENING THE COLD CASE

October 16, 2017

In October of 2017, as a founder and two-year member of the Special Victims DNA Cold Case Squad, I was assigned to reopen and reinvestigate Jane Doe's case. Since its inception in 2015, the Squad has been composed of a hand-selected group of one supervisor and six investigators from Manhattan, Brooklyn, Queens, and the Bronx. This specialized unit was created to focus on unsolved sexual assault cases where DNA evidence was available but had not yet led to an identification of the perpetrator. Every member of our dedicated team was fueled by the commitment to resolve long-standing cases and to bring justice to victims who had waited years for closure.

Jane Doe's case had long run cold since Tuesday, April 26, 1994, the day of her sexual assault by a stranger who was never caught for the crime he committed against her. Over twenty-three years had elapsed, and for all Jane Doe knew, the man who'd attacked her could still be at large, committing similar crimes against other women. Jane Doe, who was beleaguered by fears commonly shared by others who are also trauma survivors, including hypervigilance, increased anxiety, and the inability to feel safe in public, received no closure. While a defining part of survivorship is embracing the courage to live each day as an act of recovery, being saddled with the uncertainty that comes with an unresolved case often continues to manifest in numerous ways to debilitating effects, severely limiting a victim's quality of life impact a survivor's health, emotional well-being, and relationships.

The opportunity to reopen a case that had remained unsolved for over two decades had the potential to bring Jane Doe's perpetrator to justice and provide her with a long-awaited closure. Reopening cold case investigations like this one are crucial not only for resolving individual crimes that had long been considered unsolvable but also for linking the perpetrators of stranger rapes, who are so often serial offenders, to multiple cases.

Deputy Chief Michael J. Osgood, Sergeant Keri Thompson, and I assessed there was a strong probability, in Jane Doe's case, that her offender's DNA profile could be developed using modern DNA extraction and quantification technology. Early DNA profiling methods in the mid-1990s were being used as a forensics tool for criminal investigations, but the technology was very much in its nascency and was not a factor in Jane Doe's investigation because no DNA testing was completed from April of 1994 through January of 1995 when detectives were actively working the case. The limitations of DNA technology at that time meant that it was not routinely used in all criminal investigations, particularly in cases where other evidence was available or where the costs involved in DNA analysis were deemed prohibitive.

Back then, DNA testing and analysis was also far more time-consuming than it is today, and the admissibility of DNA evidence in court cases was still under consideration. The process of extracting, amplifying, and analyzing DNA samples was labor-intensive and required specialized equipment and expertise that was not widely available. Additionally, the legal system was still grappling with how to handle this new form of scientific evidence, leading to debates about its reliability in court proceedings.

Lack of standardization around the collection of DNA evidence in sexual assault cases may have been some of the reasons why Jane Doe's rape kit went untested despite the case's high profile, and despite the fact that a year and a half later DNA evidence would secure a conviction for the rapes her attacker committed in a four-month crime spree targeting other female victims from August to December of 1995. The high cost of DNA testing at the time, coupled with the absence of standardized protocols for collecting and processing DNA evidence in sexual assault cases, likely contributed to the decision not to test Jane Doe's rape kit immediately. By January 1995, lacking any new leads, the powers that be closed Jane Doe's rape case, after deciding that it was unlikely they would identify and find the perpetrator of Jane Doe's savage attack in the near term. This decision reflects the limitations of investigative techniques available at the time and the challenges faced by law enforcement in solving cases without the benefit of advanced forensic tools that are commonplace today. Six-and-a-half years after the fact, in September of 2001, as part of the NYPD Rape Kit Backlog Project, a swab from Jane's rape kit was tested for DNA, but the sample was unusable, because it had degraded, and unsuccessful in yielding a complete DNA profile of her offender.

After McAlary's third column hit newsstands, fueling Jane's umbrage that she needed to take legal action, Jane expressed a desire to return to Prospect Park, the scene of the crime, perhaps as a way to reclaim the space and confront her fears. However, an overriding sense of terror kept her from doing so. This internal conflict between wanting to face the trauma and feeling overwhelmed by crippling fear is a common experience for survivors of sexual assault. Because revisiting the location of the violation is so triggering emotionally, avoidant behavior is a common reaction among trauma survivors and a key symptom of Post-Traumatic Stress Disorder. The setting where the crime occurred has become associated with fear and powerlessness and remains the epicenter of danger in the survivor's mind, evoking intense physiological and psychological responses. While avoidance may provide a survivor with a protective sense of short-term relief, prolonged avoidance can reinforce anxieties and fears, potentially leading to a more restricted life and increased difficulty for the survivor to carry out activities of daily life.

Had the collection of DNA sampling and the usage of databases to compare DNA profiles derived from evidence with existing DNA profiles of known convicted offenders been a fully implemented resource back in 1994, Jane Doe's attacker would likely have been apprehended much sooner as he was a serial rapist who was reporting to a parole officer after having served a two-decade sentence for crimes of the same nature. The lack of a comprehensive DNA database system at that time highlights the significant advancements in forensic technology and law enforcement practices that have occurred in the time since which have made higher conviction rates and the prevention of future offenses possible.

During Jane Doe's initial investigation, the semen stains were never tested for DNA and were only tested for physical evidence of rape. The findings confirmed the presence of the p30 antigen, a protein secretion found in seminal fluid. Though the cases of the other sexual assault survivors who were attacked by the same perpetrator in the latter part of 1995 would benefit from DNA testing, limited testing reflected the standard practices of the time. Forensics focused more on confirming the occurrence of sexual contact rather than identifying the specific perpetrator through DNA analysis. While the presence of the p30 antigen confirmed sexual activity and could provide physical evidence to support prosecution, it did not provide the individualized identification that DNA profiling offers with a high degree of certainty.

As of 2012,[1] DNA samples are collected by mandate for offenders convicted of a felony-level offense or three penal law misdemeanors in the state of New York. Their DNA profile is then added to the Convicted Offender Index, COI, which is part of a software databasing suite managed by the FBI known as CODIS, the Combined DNA Index System, which supports three databases at the local, state, and national level, called LDIS, SDIS, and NDIS, respectively.

At the local level, LDIS allows individual laboratories to manage and compare DNA profiles within their jurisdiction. At the state level, SDIS facilitates data sharing among different law enforcement agencies within a state. At the national level, NDIS, enables interstate comparisons and collaborations, creating a powerful tool for tracking and identifying offenders who may cross state lines. This hierarchical structure allows for efficient sharing and comparison of DNA profiles across different jurisdictions, enhancing the ability of law enforcement agencies to solve crimes and identify suspects. The implementation of CODIS has significantly improved the capabilities of forensic investigations, allowing for the rapid matching of DNA profiles from crime scenes with those of known offenders, as well as linking DNA evidence from multiple crime scenes to identify serial offenders who might otherwise go unnoticed.

CODIS started as a pilot project in 1990 and became formalized by the DNA Identification Act of 1994, which gave the FBI the authority to develop the database that would become CODIS. This initial pilot phase involved fourteen state and local laboratories, serving as a proof of concept for the broader implementation of a national DNA database system. The act not only provided the legal framework for the FBI to establish CODIS but also set forth guidelines for the types of DNA profiles that could be included in the system, such as those from convicted offenders.

Over the next four years, software was better developed so the database would run flawlessly, standards were defined and instated, and an ambitious plan to coordinate crime labs nationally was underway. This period was crucial for refining the CODIS software, ensuring its reliability and efficiency in handling large volumes of DNA profile data. The development of standards was important, as it established protocols for DNA collection, analysis, and data entry, ensuring consistency and reliability across participating laboratories. The coordination of crime labs on a national scale was a complex undertaking, requiring extensive collaboration between federal, state, and local law enforcement agencies.

NDIS, the National DNA Index System, which is an essential part of the CODIS database, was operating at full scale by October of 1998. The period between the initial pilot project and the full-scale operation of NDIS represents a developmental phase in the evolution of forensic DNA technology, during which time many cases, including Jane Doe's, in 1994, may have missed the benefits of this powerful investigative tool.

Other indexes that have been added to CODIS in the time since its inception in the 1990s include the Forensic Index, FI, which catalogs DNA profiles from evidence found at the scene of a crime. This index plays a crucial role in modern forensic investigations, allowing law enforcement to store and compare DNA profiles obtained from various crime scenes. The Forensic Index can help identify potential links between different crimes, even when no suspect has been identified, by matching DNA profiles from multiple crime scenes. This capability is valuable in solving cold cases involving serial offenders.

The Forensic Index has become an essential tool in the arsenal of law enforcement agencies, significantly enhancing their ability to solve complex and long-standing cases. By storing DNA profiles from crime scenes, it creates a repository of genetic evidence that can be cross-referenced with other CODIS indexes, such as the Convicted Offender Index, COI. This cross-referencing capability allows investigators to potentially match crime scene DNA with profiles of known offenders providing crucial leads in investigations. Moreover, the Forensic Index has proven particularly effective in cases where traditional investigative methods have been exhausted. In situations where eyewitness testimony is lacking or physical evidence is limited, the ability to match DNA profiles from different crime scenes can provide investigators with valuable connections that might otherwise be overlooked. The FI has had a significant impact on cold case investigations as many unsolved cases from years or even decades ago can now be reinvigorated through the modern analysis of preserved DNA evidence.

Very often, solving cases involving stranger rapes comes down to findings that are DNA dependent, and having such indexed resources available in recent years dramatically enhanced the efficacy of investigations. A boon for forensic science, the CODIS software can match identical DNA profiles to separate crimes committed in different locations across differing time spans. This capability has proven invaluable in linking seemingly unrelated cases and uncovering patterns of serial offenses. The availability of comprehensive DNA databases has revolutionized the approach to solving stranger rape cases, providing investigators with tools to identify suspects who might otherwise remain unknown, which not only apprehends serial offenders who may be on the roam and eluding capture more rapidly but this powerful resource may also curb crime. Candidates who are potential suspects can be quickly identified making all the difference in the initial stages of an investigation when there is the greatest chance of building a strong case. This rapid identification process can significantly accelerate investigations of stranger rape cases by providing investigators with potential suspects early in the process. DNA databases allow for a more focused and efficient use of resources. Unlike reported cases of acquaintance and domestic rapes, where the perpetrator's identity is known to the victim, in stranger rape the perpetrator's identity is wholly unknown. Without a known suspect, traditional investigative techniques such as interviewing acquaintances or establishing motives may be of limited use. DNA evidence, however, can provide a direct link between the crime scene and the perpetrator, regardless of whether there is any prior connection between the victim and the assailant.

As the DNA databases have expanded and become comprehensive with the passage of time, more suspect and offender profiles have been added to the databases, and the odds of years-old crime scene evidence from an unsolved cold case being tested for the first time, or retested, and matching to a more recently added profile increase substantially. The successful hit rates for unsolved cold cases make a compelling argument for testing or retesting all cold cases on a periodic timetable. This access to information is a formidable way to solve cases and bring rape survivors, who are still marked by the past trauma, much-needed closure.

And while such databases can serve as a powerful tool to enhance public safety, there's a counterargument, a rising chorus of dissent about the usage and relative good of such vast reservoirs of information, from the perspective of insiders who helped to build the databases. This internal critique from those involved in the development of DNA databases highlights concerns that may not be immediately apparent to outside observers.

The ethical implications of maintaining large-scale genetic databases are profound and those in the position to know are questioning the ethical usage and relative good of compiling genetic information, raising legitimate concerns around infringements of privacy, civil liberties, and individual rights. The existence of such databasing technology increases police reliance and FBI oversight of its storehoused data, casting the potential of their becoming overly reliant on genetic evidence at the risk of neglecting other tried and true investigative methods. Additionally, the centralization of such sensitive data raises concerns about the potential for misuse or unauthorized access. This is at the very center of ongoing policy discussions about how such tools should be used ethically when it comes to law enforcement and the criminal justice system. Proponents argue that the benefits of expanded DNA collection in terms of public safety and justice outweigh the potential risks. They point to numerous cases where DNA evidence has not only helped convict the guilty but also exonerated the innocent, highlighting its role in enhancing the accuracy and fairness of the criminal justice system and driving reform.

Should the rapid growth of DNA databases, designed in part to increase public safety, ever be retooled for purposes far removed from the original intent, for instance, widespread genetic surveillance, such misappropriation and misuse may be very difficult for privacy advocates and legal minds to regulate. Full-blown genetic surveillance would infringe on personal privacy and civil liberties in ways that were not anticipated when these databases were first established. The challenge of regulating such powerful technological tools necessitates public discourse on policy about imposing appropriate limits on collecting genetic data.

Dr. Howard Baum, formerly the Deputy Director of the Forensic Biology laboratory in the New York City Chief Medical Examiner's Office, built the local database in 1997, then called Linkage, in the time before it merged with LDIS in 2014. Baum's expertise in forensic science and his role in the Chief Medical Examiner's Office positioned him well to spearhead this initiative, which predated the widespread adoption of such databases across the country.

The city database, or "The Local," as detectives often refer to it today, was designed to assist law enforcement, though it is officially maintained by the New York City Office of the Chief Medical Examiner rather than the NYPD. Having the OCME manage a law enforcement tool, reflects the specialized nature of DNA analysis and the need for scientific integrity in maintaining forensic databases. "The Local" merged with LDIS, the Local DNA Index System, in 2014 which likely allowed for better integration with state and national DNA databases.

While the OCME has standards for its DNA testing, Dr. Baum, in more recent years, has joined the growing number of concerned voices who claim the surreptitious collection practices around DNA sampling have resulted in a rogue and lawless database that warehouses the genetic profiles of arrestees and minors who have never been convicted of a crime. This shift in perspective, from creator to critic, underscores the ethical concerns surrounding DNA collection and storage practices. Depending on eligibility requirements, profiles from LDIS are uploaded to SDIS (the state database) and NDIS (the national database), both of which are regulated, but there is little to no accountability about what remains in "The Local," sometimes for years, casting the specter of criminality on individuals, some of whom are unaware their DNA was ever collected in connection with criminal investigations.

Dr. Baum believes the local database he helped to get underway during his tenure with the OCME's Forensic Biology Department has inflated well beyond its intended purpose with 82,000 DNA profiles as of 2020 in three discrete local indices—a missing persons index, a crime scene evidence index, and a suspect profile index. The sheer volume of the number of profiles stored raises questions about the necessity of such extensive data collection. This expansion of the database far beyond its original scope highlights the potential for "function creep," where systems initially designed for a specific purpose gradually expand to serve broader functions without adequate public scrutiny or debate.

Thirty-eight percent of the total are 32,000 profiles stored in the suspect profile index, inclusive of those individuals who have never been convicted of a crime. Unchecked, this could easily transfigure into the unwarranted surveillance and investigation of innocent individuals. While these databases can be powerful tools for solving crimes and exonerating the innocent, their rapid growth without corresponding increases in oversight and safeguards poses significant risks to privacy and civil liberties. As these databases grow larger, they become more attractive targets for hackers or unauthorized access. The sensitive nature of genetic information makes the event of an invasive breach concerning, as it could reveal sensitive information not just about an individual but also about biological relatives.

Before collecting an individual's DNA, his or her valid and explicit consent must be obtained via the submission of a "Consent to Submit DNA Sample" form, which also includes their right to refusal. This requirement for explicit consent is a crucial safeguard for individual privacy rights and bodily autonomy, ensuring that individuals are fully informed about the purpose of the DNA collection and have the opportunity to make a conscious decision about their participation. The inclusion of the right to refuse on the consent form is important, as it clearly states that DNA collection is not mandatory and emphasizes individuals' power to decline. When consent is granted, usually a buccal swab or a saliva sample is expedient for the express purpose of collection. Both are noninvasive collection methods designed to minimize physical discomfort while obtaining a viable DNA sample. Otherwise, barring consent, a court order, or a warrant is needed, underscores the protected status of genetic information. The need for judicial oversight in the absence of consent provides a layer of protection against potential overreach by law enforcement agencies.

New York state law which guarantees search and seizure protections does not extend to samples that are considered "abandoned." This legal loophole regarding abandoned DNA samples has become a contentious issue in the debate over genetic privacy rights as the concept of abandoned DNA challenges traditional notions of privacy and ownership of genetic material. The definition of what constitutes "abandoned" DNA can be ambiguous and open to interpretation, stretching the generally accepted meaning in collection practices of abandonment samples.

There is undeniably a gray area at the intersection of explicit consent and the furtive collection practice of DNA samples, resulting in expediency without due process. This practice of collecting abandoned DNA samples circumvents established protections against unreasonable search and seizure. It conceivably undermines the Fourth Amendment protections against unreasonable searches, as this practice raises questions about whether individuals have "a reasonable expectation of privacy" in their discarded genetic material. The testing and analysis of "abandoned" DNA of an individual, guilty or innocent, reveals highly sensitive personal information, such as ancestry or preexisting genetic conditions, that is often far more specific than what is needed to corroborate the findings of a criminal investigation.

If detectives establish probable cause and an arrest is made, the arrestee who is named as a suspect can be brought into the precinct. While being questioned in a sanitized interrogation room, an object such as a water bottle from which the suspect drank can become a biological sample retained for DNA testing. This seemingly innocuous act of offering a drink to a suspect, while appearing courteous, is a calculated move. This practice of covert DNA collection during interrogations raises significant ethical concerns which violate the spirit, if not the letter, of laws designed to protect individual privacy rights, unjustly circumventing the requirement to receive written consent from the arrestee or the requirement to obtain a warrant. Law enforcement's use of this arguably deceptive tactic to obtain a DNA sample without explicit consent or a warrant entirely undermines the notion of informed consent, an ethical practice which ensures individuals are fully aware of and agree to procedures which involve their personal information or biological samples. Moreover, the surreptitious nature of this collection method challenges fundamental principles of transparency and fairness in the criminal justice system.

Typically, abandonment samples would be classified as the trace amounts of DNA left behind at a crime scene, not DNA extracted from water bottles left in interrogation rooms which far stretches the meaning of the word "abandoned." This absurd interpretation of what constitutes "abandoned" DNA blurs the lines between legitimate evidence collection and potential violations of privacy rights, exploiting a legal loophole. Though the DNA profile associated with the arrest can only be compared to evidence directly related to the case, the profile languishes in the local database with little being done in the way of routine expungement protocols. This prolonged retention increases the risk of misuse, unauthorized access, or future expansion of the profile's use beyond its original, case-specific purpose.

Among communities of color who are already subject to profiling practices that disproportionately affect them, such surreptitious collection can result in an overcollection of data, exacerbating existing inequalities in the criminal justice system and undermining trust in law enforcement. The broad retention of DNA profiles is stigmatizing, resulting in the increased surveillance of certain populations with existing disparities and historically higher conviction rates. The social cost of casting the specter of criminality over whole swathes of communities, and the individuals who comprise them, irredeemably perpetuates systemic bias and discrimination based on a person's DNA profiles rather than his or her actions, raising red flags about equal protection violations.

DNA profiles in the New York State DNA Databank, created in 1994 following the passage of legislation and operational by 1996, are managed by the New York State Division of Criminal Justice Services. This databank represents a significant tool in law enforcement efforts, allowing for the storage and comparison of genetic information to aid in criminal investigations.

Profiles in this databank are regularly integrated into SDIS, the State DNA Index System, which forms part of the hierarchical structure of DNA databases in the United States. This integration allows for broader searches and comparisons across state lines, enhancing the effectiveness of DNA-based investigative techniques.

As of 2012, the New York State DNA Databank contains profiles of convicted offenders of any New York felony-level offenses or penal law misdemeanor. This catch-all had begun as a series of expansions since the database's inception. The expansion of the database's scope reflects the evolving approach to DNA collection in criminal justice systems, with a trend toward more comprehensive coverage driven by advancements in DNA technology.

In 1996, it was only offenders convicted of certain crimes that had their DNA collected, but gradually the number of offenses steadily ballooned to include all felony offenses or penal law misdemeanors despite strict state law regulations regarding the permanent storage of profiles of identified individuals, who either needed to qualify as convicted known offenders or those added by court order. This expansion has been a subject of debate while the evolution of the New York State DNA Databank reflects broader trends in the use of genetic information in criminal justice systems across the United States.

NDIS allows for the sharing of DNA profiles across state lines, enhancing the capabilities of law enforcement in solving crimes. Over time, both federal and state laws have expanded to allow for the inclusion of more profiles. However, this expansion has courted controversy and remains a contentious issue, as with the other indexed databases, in the ongoing dispute over DNA databases and their use in law enforcement.

Speaking out in defense of their practices, the OCME maintains that 75 percent of its 32,000 profiles in the suspect profile index of New York's local database also have a profile in SDIS which suggests the same individual has been convicted of a crime at some point in time. This statistic is presented as a justification for the retention of suspect profiles, implying that a significant majority of individuals in the local database have a criminal history that warrants their inclusion. The OCME likely views this as evidence that their practices are largely targeting individuals with a history of criminal activity, rather than indiscriminately collecting DNA from innocent citizens.

The existence of overlapping profiles between local and state databases does not inherently justify the retention of all profiles at the local level, especially considering the potential for more lenient inclusion criteria in local databases compared to state or national ones. While reassuring in part, this statistic does not obviate the need to have stricter controls and protocols at the local level in New York City, to ensure that the collection, retention, and use of DNA profiles adhere to legal and ethical standards, regardless of the overlap with SDIS. While the cited 75 percent of overlap with SDIS profiles provides some legitimacy to the local database practices, the remaining 25 percent of profiles that do not have a corresponding entry in the state database potentially represent those individuals who have never been convicted of a crime. Twenty-five percent is a significant minority as retention of DNA profiles for individuals not convicted of crimes presents ethical and legal challenges.

The need for stricter protocols at the local level is unquestionably necessary as the risk and threat of misuse or unauthorized access to sensitive genetic information necessitates robust safeguards, regardless of the composition of the database. A lack of comprehensive and standardized protocols breeds inconsistencies in how DNA data continues to be collected and stored which, if poorly regulated, will result in unequal treatment under the law, violating individuals' constitutional rights.

One way the NYPD and OCME are working in tandem to legitimize and improve upon what Dr. Baum called its "half-baked policies" is to audit every suspect profile that has been in the local database for two years or more with the commitment to review all profiles automatically at the two-year marker. This initiative represents a significant step toward addressing concerns about the long-term retention of DNA profiles and the potential infringement on individual privacy rights. By implementing regular audits, the NYPD and OCME are demonstrating a commitment to maintaining the integrity of the database while also respecting the civil liberties of those whose DNA profiles are stored. The two-year review cycle provides a structured solution to managing the database, potentially preventing the indefinite retention of profiles that may no longer be relevant to active investigations.

Such a review process acknowledges the sensitive nature of genetic information and the need for safeguards against potential abuses of this powerful investigative tool by providing a mechanism for removing profiles, reducing the risk of misuse. Despite the potential for abuse, when used responsibly, "The Local" can be a valuable asset in solving complex cases and serve to enhance investigators' ability to identify a broader pool of potential suspects in complex cases where the perpetrator's identity remains unknown. The implementation of regular audits and review processes is a step in the right direction. Over the long term, ongoing vigilance and transparency are necessary to ensure that the database is used ethically. The effectiveness and fairness of the audit process itself should be subject to periodic review and adjustment as needed. Transparency in reporting the outcomes of these audits, including the number of profiles removed and the reasons for retention, can further enhance public confidence in the system.

Clear guidelines regarding the criteria for inclusion in the database, and the duration of profile retention still need to be formalized and enforced. These guidelines should be developed with input from various stakeholders, including legal experts, civil rights advocates, and forensic scientists. They should address issues such as the threshold for inclusion in the database, the process for removing profiles, and the rights of individuals to request removal of their profiles. Additionally, there should be clear protocols for handling profiles of individuals who have been exonerated or whose charges have been dismissed.

Jane Doe's assailant had been released on parole in 1993 after serving a two-decade prison sentence from 1973 to 1993 for earlier stranger rapes committed in four different precincts in the New York area from 1968 to 1973. His history of serial offenses underscores the importance of tracking and monitoring convicted sex offenders, especially those with a pattern of stranger assaults. The fact that he had committed crimes across multiple precincts highlights the challenges law enforcement faced in connecting related cases before the advent of centralized DNA databases. This pattern of cross-jurisdictional offenses exemplifies the difficulties investigators encountered in identifying serial offenders who operated in different areas, as each precinct might have been working in relative isolation without the benefit of a unified system to link similar crimes.

After his release, he would have been documented on a parolee list as a sex offender, but in the mid-1990s when Detective Sorrentino was first investigating the case, tracking down such confirmation may have been a laborious process. The limitations of information sharing and record-keeping systems in the mid-1990s created significant obstacles for investigators like Sorrentino trying to identify potential suspects. These constraints in data management and interagency communication often resulted in crucial information being siloed within individual precincts or departments, making it challenging to establish connections between seemingly unrelated cases or to identify patterns in criminal behavior across different jurisdictions.

While there have been dramatic improvements in data management and accessibility to information since the mid-1990s, at the time Sorrentino would likely have had to make an in-person trip to the parole office, sort through a log book with a hard copy list of parolees, with the tedious task of sifting through its handwritten documentation, all while pressure to solve the case was mounting as Jane Doe's credibility was ensnared in tabloid fodder. This manual process of information retrieval was not only time-consuming but also prone to human error, potentially leading to overlooked connections or missed opportunities in the investigation. The reliance on physical records and in-person visits to various offices for information gathering meant that investigations were often bottlenecked by administrative tasks, diverting valuable time and resources from active fieldwork and analysis. This inefficient system also made it difficult to quickly cross-reference information from different sources. The digitization of these formerly analog systems, as well as the implementation of DNA databases, was a game-changer.

By 2007, a Parolee Offender Database was developed that gave detectives access to a digitally compiled list of parolees. This advancement was a significant improvement in law enforcement's ability to track and monitor parolees, particularly those convicted of serious offenses like sexual assault. A detective could type in a search for a parolee offender by precinct, name, and New York State ID number. The creation of such a database streamlined the process of identifying potential suspects, vastly improving upon the manual, time-consuming methods of the past. The ability to quickly filter and sort through parolee data based on various criteria and cross-reference parolee information across precincts enhanced the efficiency and effectiveness of investigations, especially in cases involving repeat offenders. This cross-precinct functionality allowed for a more comprehensive view of an individual's criminal history across different jurisdictions.

A photo can be obtained through the Department of Motor Vehicles, and depending on the circumstances, if there are photos that closely resemble the sketch provided by the victim, a photo array is put together for purposes of identification. This integration of various data sources, including DMV records, demonstrates the increasing interconnectedness of law enforcement databases and information systems. The ability to quickly access and utilize DMV photographs in conjunction with parolee data represents a significant advancement in the tools available to investigators, saving time in the early stages of an investigation when leads are fresh.

Compared to earlier methods, the use of photo arrays based on the victim's description and official photographs represents a more systematic and potentially more reliable approach to identifying a suspect.

If a rape victim identifies who she believes is the perpetrator, it is usually grounds for arrest, though eyewitness testimony can at times be fallible. While victim identification remains integral to many investigations, there is the pragmatic need to corroborate such identifications with other forms of evidence whenever possible. Pursuing investigative pathways to physically track down the offender can mean canvassing shelters, halfway houses, and other locations in and around the area where the crime occurred. This traditional approach to locating suspects is evergreen, and a critical aspect of on-the-ground, community-based police work, even as access to better data-driven technology streamlines the time spent on investigations.

Because of the high rate of recidivism for serial rapists committing sex crimes, it only takes one sex conviction to qualify for DNA collection, reflecting the persistent threat posed by repeat sexual offenders and the value of DNA evidence in identifying and apprehending these individuals. An offender's DNA profile, once uploaded to a database, has the potential match to multiple crimes by the same offender, resolving cold cases from the past, sometimes decades after the original crime occurred, as with Jane Doe, as well as serial offenses in the future. This attests to the inherent value of maintaining comprehensive DNA databases over the long term, though critics are quick to cite that no system is infallible and there's always the potential misuse of genetic information both practically and ethically. As the size of DNA databases grows, so does the statistical likelihood of coincidental false matches underscores the importance of using DNA evidence in conjunction with other forms of evidence, rather than as a standalone proof of guilt.

For cases that have gone cold due to lack of leads or evidence, a DNA match can breathe new life into the investigation, offering hope for victims and their families who have long-awaited resolution. Moreover, the potential to link a DNA profile to future offenses can serve as a deterrent as well, discouraging some offenders who know that their DNA is on file potentially reducing recidivism rates in certain categories of crime. Should they choose to reoffend, DNA evidence will significantly increase the likelihood of their identification and apprehension.

Jane Doe's attacker's DNA was collected on January 22, 1998, in the time after he'd assaulted her in April of 1994 in Prospect Park. This multi-year gap between Jane's assault and her perpetrator's DNA collection highlights the challenges faced by law enforcement in identifying and apprehending perpetrators of stranger rape. While the identity of Jane's perpetrator would remain unidentified for many years, he had been convicted and re-incarcerated in October of 1997 in connection with four other cases of rape consistent with the perpetrator's modus operandi from August 17, 1995, to December 4, 1995. The fact that the perpetrator continued to commit felony-level sex offenses after Jane Doe's assault emphasizes the critical role that timely DNA analysis and database matching can play in preventing further victimization.

The perpetrator's DNA sample was uploaded to CODIS on July 25, 2000, more than two and a half years after the collection date. This administrative lag between DNA collection and CODIS upload, attributed to staffing shortages and insufficient budgets to fund such efforts consistently, exemplifies the challenges faced by forensic laboratories with keeping CODIS up-to-date. Giving serial offenders the opportunity to commit more crimes, while eluding DNA identification, the backlog in processing and uploading DNA samples was a widespread issue that hampered the effectiveness of what these DNA databases were designed to do in helping to solve crimes and identify repeat offenders. Federally funded programs such as the DNA Capacity Enhancement for Backlog Reductions help states to address the backlog. These initiatives recognize the vital importance of maintaining up-to-date and comprehensive DNA databases. By providing resources to increase laboratory capacity and efficiency, these programs aim to reduce the backlog and improve the timeliness of DNA analysis and database uploads.

Since 2006, there was a notable change in New York's criminal law when it eliminated the statute of limitations on first-degree rape cases.

This legal reform recognized the severity of sex crimes and the challenges victims often face in reporting and pursuing justice. The elimination of the statute of limitations provided rape victims with more time to come forward and allowed law enforcement to prosecute these cases regardless of when they occurred.

For Jane Doe, who was raped in 1994, seeking prosecution would have been a race against the clock, as the statute of limitations was five years from the date the crime was committed. The limited timeframe placed immense pressure on law enforcement to gather evidence and build a case quickly and failed to account for the psychological burden Jane endured from both her sexual assault and the media notoriety of being disbelieved. The five-year statute of limitations in place at the time of Jane Doe's assault likely represented a significant barrier to justice for many sexual assault survivors, who, like Jane, were racing against the same clock. Given the complex psychological and emotional processes that survivors undergo, many may have delayed beyond the point of being able to prosecute. Given that Jane Doe's case went unsolved, justice was delayed and the hope for swift prosecution was denied her.

The change in law in 2006, while too late to directly impact Jane Doe's case, was a significant and progressive step in how our legal system adjudicates rape cases. An elimination of the statute of limitations grants victims the time they need and also allows evidence collected from a crime scene in years past to benefit from modern advances in forensic technology.

Had there been no backlog and had her perpetrator's DNA sample been uploaded immediately after collection in January of 1998, Jane's rape kit would also have needed to have been tested for DNA evidence, and the DNA collected would have needed to have been sufficient to obtain a profile eligible to upload to CODIS in order to obtain a match. Jane's rape kit was tested for DNA in September of 2001, when there was a renewed interest in clearing the backlog for DNA testing of rape kits from outstanding cold cases. This delay of over seven years between the assault and the DNA testing of the rape kit underscores the significant backlog issues faced by many jurisdictions. Unfortunately, there was no usable evidence for a match from the contents of the kit, and Jane Doe did not benefit from the sea change in legislation in 2006 as the changes in the law did not apply retroactively to her case since no DNA evidence had been discovered.

The inability to apply the 2006 legislative changes retroactively to Jane Doe's case highlights a common challenge in legal reforms: balancing the desire for justice with principles of legal certainty and fairness. While the elimination of the statute of limitations for first-degree rape cases was a significant step forward, its nonretroactive application meant that many victims of older crimes, like Jane Doe, did not benefit, having the unintended effect of compounding the sense of injustice experienced by these victims.

American feminist and author Susan Brownmiller, well known for her 1975 book *Against Our Will: Men, Women, and Rape*, challenged prevailing myths about rape and helped to reframe sexual assault as a crime of power and violence rather than passion. She noted that the change in the statute of limitations in 2006, which benefits survivors is, "more important now because of DNA. You can eventually find the guy who couldn't be found by other means."[2] Her observation underscores the potential of DNA evidence to solve cases that might have gone cold under previous legal time constraints, recognizing genetic evidence as a powerful tool in criminal investigations. Brownmiller points to a synergy between legal reform and scientific advancement, which delivers new hope for survivors of sexual assault, potentially providing avenues for justice that were previously unattainable. By emphasizing the importance of DNA evidence in conjunction with the extended statute of limitations, Brownmiller acknowledges the evolving landscape of criminal justice and its potential to address long-standing challenges in prosecuting sexual assault cases.

Sheldon Silver, who formerly served as the Speaker of the New York State Assembly poignantly stated in a press release in 2006, when the law changed, "Rape and sexual assault are heinous crimes that forever affect survivors. Many survivors are so traumatized that they cannot immediately report their crimes. This legislation seeks to leave the window of opportunity open for any victim to seek justice in a time frame that is dictated by their needs and not an arbitrary timetable set by the criminal justice system."[3] This victim-centered approach to justice reflects a significant cultural shift in our more nuanced and compassionate understanding of sex crimes and the long-term trauma associated with sexual assault and the various factors that may delay reporting by victims. The 2006 legislation which eliminated the statute of limitations for first-degree rape cases in New York was a landmark change that addressed long-standing concerns about the barriers faced by sexual assault survivors in seeking justice.

There has been some grumbling from defense attorneys who argue that statutes are in place for good reason, such as the unreliability of aging recollections by witnesses[4] and the degradation of key evidence. There's a general consensus among defense attorneys that there needs to be some defined period after which the accused can no longer be indicted, as defendants should not have to live indefinitely under the threat of prosecution. This perspective highlights the tension between the desire for justice for victims and the need to ensure fair trials for the accused that maintain their presumption of innocence until proven guilty. There are legitimate concerns the passage of time can have on quality and availability of evidence, potentially compromising the integrity of the legal process. Defense attorneys often argue that as time passes, witnesses may no longer be available to testify or the reliability of eyewitness testimony, by the aggrieved and by other witnesses, can significantly diminish as memories fade. In addition, the loss of exculpatory evidence could potentially result in wrongful convictions. These factors can make it more challenging to build a strong defense. If key evidence that could exonerate an accused person is no longer available due to the passage of time, it could lead to miscarriages of justice.

Those in praise of the change in the law that abolished the statute of limitations cite the severity of first-degree rape and equally venal sex crimes in which perpetrators should be held accountable regardless of when the crime occurred. Proponents argue that the heinous nature of these crimes warrants special consideration in the legal system, justifying the removal of time constraints on prosecution. They contend that allowing perpetrators to escape justice merely due to the passage of time undermines the principles of accountability and public safety. Many survivors experience post-traumatic stress disorder, depression, anxiety, and other mental health challenges that can delay their ability or willingness to engage with the criminal justice system. By removing the statute of limitations, the law provides survivors with the time they may need to process their trauma and come forward when they feel ready and able to do so.

DNA analysis makes solving and prosecuting cold cases with the outcome of higher conviction rates possible. Providing crucial leads in cases that might otherwise have gone unsolved, DNA evidence can offer compelling proof of guilt or innocence in court. The advancement of DNA technology has, while not infallible, nonetheless revolutionized the investigation and prosecution of sexual assault cases, yielding a level of certainty of evidence that was previously unattainable in many instances. The ability to analyze DNA samples years or even decades after a crime was committed has opened up new possibilities for achieving justice in cold cases.

The elimination of the statute of limitations sends a powerful message to both survivors and perpetrators. For survivors, it validates their experiences and communicates that society is committed to pursuing justice on their behalf, regardless of when they feel ready to come forward. For perpetrators, it serves as a deterrent, signaling that the passage of time will not shield them from accountability for their actions. By removing arbitrary time limits on prosecution, the law aligns more closely with the lived experiences of survivors, in acknowledgment of the ongoing nature of the harm caused by sexual violence.

In the time before the statute of limitations was eliminated, rape survivors who were willing to testify before a grand jury would allow prosecutors to create what is called a "John Doe" indictment[5] to stop the clock. This legal strategy emerged as a creative solution to the challenges posed by statutes of limitations in cases where the perpetrator's identity remained unknown. It provided a lifeline for cases that might otherwise have been rendered unprosecutable due to the passage of time, offering hope to survivors and law enforcement alike.

These indictments were used for stranger rapes that had male DNA profiles eligible to be cataloged in CODIS, even though the identity of the suspect was still unknown at the time of the indictment. This innovative legal strategy provided a way to preserve the possibility of future prosecution in cases where the perpetrator's identity remained a mystery and demonstrated how the criminal justice system adapted to leverage new scientific capabilities in the pursuit of justice. By indicting the DNA profile itself, prosecutors could effectively pause the statute of limitations, giving law enforcement more time to identify and apprehend the suspect, acknowledging the potential for DNA evidence to solve these cases, even years after the crime occurred.

As the Manhattan District Attorney's Office began doing this it inspired other boroughs to follow suit, and many unsolved cases were reopened as a result in the hopes that there would be DNA hits that properly identified these assailants in the future. This approach spread rapidly across New York City, demonstrating its potential to address long-standing issues with cold cases and unresolved sexual assaults.

Dr. Howard Baum, who was subsequently the Director of the New Jersey State Police Forensic Science Laboratory, following his tenure with the New York City Chief Medical Examiner's office, remarked, "You are indicting the DNA profile, not the person," encapsulating the essence of the John Doe indictment strategy which departs from the traditional person-centered indictments, focusing instead on using scientific evidence as the basis for legal action. By focusing on the genetic evidence rather than a named individual, prosecutors could maintain the legal validity of their case while continuing to search for the person matching that DNA profile, highlighting its potential as a powerful tool in the pursuit of justice. This innovation not only preserved the possibility of future prosecution but also underscored the indispensable application of forensic evidence in criminal investigation, bridging scientific and legal realms in a way not seen before.

The use of John Doe indictments represents a significant shift in how the criminal justice system approaches cold cases, particularly those involving sexual assault. Such possibilities also confront an increasing reliance on scientific evidence in criminal investigations and prosecutions, as well as the legal system's adaptability in the face of technological advancements. Moreover, while the use of John Doe indictments offers new hope for solving cold cases, it also challenges traditional notions of due process and the right to a speedy trial as constitutionally guaranteed. Due process typically requires notice and the opportunity to be heard. When the identity of the perpetrator is unknown at the time of the John Doe indictment, the line that ensures the rights of the accused are being adequately protected becomes blurred. In addition, a significant delay between the time of an indictment, the time an arrest is made, and the date a trial is set is arguably a violation of the constitutional right to a speedy trial.

As of 2000, a year after Jane Doe's five-year time period for prosecution had expired, her assaulter's DNA profile was in CODIS but just sat there, as no crime scene evidence related to Jane Doe's case was ever DNA tested. The presence of the assailant's DNA profile in CODIS without a corresponding test of Jane Doe's evidence gathered from the rape kit or at the crime scene represents a missed opportunity for justice to prevail, and a critical gap in how the investigation unfolded, attesting to the importance of comprehensive and timely DNA testing in cases of sexual assault. The failure to test Jane Doe's rape kit for DNA, despite the existence of a potential match in CODIS, points to systemic deficits resulting in perhaps an arbitrary or discretionary decision as to which sexual assault cases being investigated in the mid-1990s would have the benefit of DNA analysis.

It was not until a year later in September of 2001 that Jane Doe's rape kit was tested for DNA evidence and sent out to GeneScreen Laboratory, with a flush of new funding that supported the "End the Backlog" initiative. This delay in testing, despite the availability of the assailant's DNA profile in CODIS, demonstrates the systemic issues that have plagued the processing of sexual assault evidence. The "End the Backlog" initiative was an effort to address long-standing issues of insufficient funding for forensic laboratories and a lack of trained personnel to process evidence, to better ensure that rape kits are tested promptly and thoroughly. The backlog of untested rape kits has been infamously a nationwide problem with hundreds of thousands of kits left untested in police evidence rooms and crime labs across the country. This initiative, spearheaded by various advocacy groups and supported by federal and state funding, aimed to significantly reduce the backlog and to implement reforms to prevent future backlogs. Efforts were focused not only on testing old kits but also on improving the entire system of responding to and investigating sexual assault cases, from evidence collection to prosecution.

However, the sample from Jane Doe's vaginal swab came back with negative results as the swab was degraded, and there was not enough DNA for a CODIS-eligible profile to be developed in an attempt to identify a suspect. The degradation of DNA in biological evidence is influenced by a number of factors, including temperature, humidity, and exposure to UV light. In the case of vaginal swabs, the presence of enzymes and bacteria can accelerate DNA degradation. While advanced forensic techniques today can maximize what is extracted from limited or degraded samples, DNA degradation of biological evidence over time can significantly impact the ability to obtain usable genetic profiles, compromising the potential to solve cases and bringing perpetrators to justice. Jane Doe's vaginal swab was entirely consumed during the testing process, which made any further analysis fruitless, nixing the possibility of retesting the sample with techniques that may be developed in the future.

In the time after I founded the Special Victims DNA Cold Case Squad, if I were working on a sexual assault and the rape kit came back negative, I'd put in a request, especially if it were a vicious case, for the victim's clothing to be tested, in recognition of the fact that valuable DNA evidence may be present in places beyond the standard contents of a rape kit. For complex sexual assault cases in which initial evidence yields limited results, this mindset to be willing to explore additional sources of DNA is essential and can lead to breaking a case. The lack of funding in the early days of DNA technology resulted in missed opportunities to solve cases and identify perpetrators, underscoring the importance of adequate resources for forensic testing. As of today, all rape kits are tested and many states are up-to-date with no significant backlog, representing a major advancement in the handling of sexual assault evidence and reflecting the success of initiatives like "End the Backlog."

The transition from rarely testing rape kits to ensuring that all kits are processed not only improves the odds of solving individual cases but also sends a powerful message to survivors that their cases are being taken seriously and that every effort is being made to achieve justice on their behalf. Prioritizing the testing of all rape kits is an important step in challenging rape culture and demonstrates a commitment to thorough and equitable treatment of sexual assault cases, regardless of the perceived likelihood of solving the crime. The elimination of significant backlogs in many states is a testament to the increased resources, improved processes, and heightened awareness surrounding the importance of timely DNA testing in sexual assault cases. This progress helps to address the historical injustices caused by untested rape kits and provides hope for survivors who may have waited years for their evidence to be processed.

Had Jane's running shorts been tested for DNA in 2001, and a CODIS-eligible sample created, it would have "hit" Jane's violator, whose profile was also in the database as of July 25, 2000. This cold case would likely have been solved in 2001, or soon after rather than going unsolved for over two decades. Advancements in methods for DNA analysis and the power of DNA databases like CODIS underscore the value of preserving and testing physical evidence, even in cases that have gone cold.

It was only in the time after I was reassigned the case in 2017 that I requested assistance from a colleague to re-voucher Jane Doe's 1994 sexual offense evidence collection kit from the Pearson Place Warehouse, the NYPD's evidence storage facility. Both the kit and the running shorts were delivered to the Office of the Chief Medical Examiner's Department of Forensic Biology for forensic examination. Of ten stains found on the running shorts, seven of the stains had no DNA, and three of the stains, labeled Stain #1, #3, and #4, were identified as having male DNA present. The discovery of male DNA on the victim's clothing, even after so many years, was a significant breakthrough in the investigation underscoring the value of re-examining evidence with modern forensic techniques.

Discovering male DNA on multiple stains provided new leads for identifying the perpetrator. Stain #4 was sufficient for direct comparison only, which would yield a very partial DNA profile as the amount of DNA extracted was low. A comparison to known DNA profiles already in the database could be made, but there wasn't enough DNA in the evidence sample for a conclusive match to a known suspect or offender. Stain #1 was a two-donor mixture of epithelial cell and sperm cell fractions, with the epithelial cells primarily from Jane Doe and the sperm cells fractions composed of male DNA, though there can be some carryover.

Back in 1994, there was a spot test using the HLA-DQ alpha polymarker which looked at genetic variation at a locus located within the human leukocyte antigen gene complex on chromosome six, referred to as the HLA system. The HLA system represented an early approach to genetic identification in forensic science, later paving the way for more advanced techniques. While this spot testing was fast, it was best used as a first step in a forensic investigation, as results were not as accurate as RFLP,[6] Restriction Fragment Length Polymorphism, the DNA testing method which was most commonly used in the early days of DNA analysis. The transition from HLA testing and RFLP to more updated techniques like PCR-based methods subsequently was indicative of the rapid advancements in forensic technology and the ongoing improvements in the accuracy and sensitivity of DNA analysis in criminal investigations.

RFLP involved restriction enzymes cleaving DNA into fragments and, through a technique called gel electrophoresis, fragments were flushed into a gel which would ultimately reveal a pattern of bands, unique to each individual, which made this method effective for profiling. While one of the earliest DNA profiling techniques used in forensic science and groundbreaking at the time, this process was complex and required a significant amount of intact DNA to yield reliable results. With enough matter, the unique banding patterns produced by RFLP analysis provided a powerful tool for individual identification. However, in cases where there was degraded or small amounts of DNA, this technique fell short.

The RFLP method's ability to create unique genetic profiles was a major step forward in forensic DNA analysis, but it was time-consuming. If Jane Doe's rape hit had been DNA tested when her case was initially investigated from April 1994 to January 1995, while a handful of forensic labs were transitioning from RFLP (Restriction Fragment Length Polymorphism) to the adoption of differential extraction techniques that could separate sperm cells from epithelial cells, methods were far less efficient than current methods used today. There was no extraction protocol developed at the time, for either the spot test or RFLP, that could separate Jane Doe's alleles from Stain #1, which was a two-donor mixture, to obtain the male profile. The inability to separate a mixed biological DNA sample, and the time-consuming nature of RFLP analysis, often led to delays in processing evidence, leaving cases unsolved.

Fortunately, methods have advanced in the time since, which can isolate the male DNA. Modern techniques, such as Y-chromosome STR analysis and more sophisticated PCR-based methods, have greatly improved the ability to isolate and analyze male DNA in mixed samples, crucial in sexual assault cases where the ability to distinguish between male and female DNA is needed to identify a male perpetrator. These newer techniques not only allow for the analysis of smaller and more degraded DNA samples but also provide faster results and greater sensitivity in detecting and isolating specific DNA profiles from mixed samples.

According to the National Research Council, PCR STR Testing is presently considered the gold standard for DNA analysis, a significant advancement in forensic DNA technology since the early days of RFLP analysis. PCR STR, Polymerase Chain Reaction Short Tandem Repeat, testing combines the amplification power of PCR with the high variability of STR markers, providing a powerful and reliable method for DNA profiling.

PCR, or Polymerase Chain Reaction technique, is a method of amplification, sometimes referred to as molecular "xeroxing," that creates copies of the original DNA segment with a high degree of fidelity. This technique revolutionized DNA analysis by allowing scientists to work with extremely small amounts of genetic material. The ability to amplify DNA samples has been essential in forensic applications, where collected evidence may be limited or degraded genetic material. While finding a needle in a haystack may be an impossible task, if you have a million xeroxed haystacks, the chances of finding the one needle you are looking for improves considerably.

This always struck me as a neat allegory as trying to investigate and track down the culprit of a stranger rape in an age before DNA evidence was routinely collected and tested, with limited physical evidence or eyewitness accounts, was likely a lot like finding a needle in a haystack.

STR, known as Short Tandem Repeats, are fragments of DNA with highly repetitive structures of 1–7 nucleotide base pairs, which can be compared to pearl beads on a necklace. The repetitive nature of STRs is key to their usefulness in forensic DNA profiling, as the number of repeats can vary significantly between individuals. The Locus, more often referred to by its plural form LOCI, is the location on the chromosome where STRs, which are genetic markers, are found. In DNA profiling, it is the LOCI that provides the specific locations on chromosomes where genetic variations are examined. These locations are carefully selected for their high variability among individuals, making them ideal for purposes of identification.

There is wide genetic variation between individuals, one person may have ten beads at a specific locus whereas another person may have five. This variation in the number of repeats at specific genetic loci among individuals allows for the creation of highly discriminating DNA profiles, enabling forensic scientists to distinguish between individuals with a high degree of certainty and statistical confidence.

For the purpose of forensic profiling, a minimum of thirteen LOCI and up to twenty LOCI or more are analyzed, and if there is a match at multiple LOCI, it's as unique as a genetic fingerprint and underscores the likelihood that two matching samples, such as an evidence sample and a collected sample already in the database, are from the same person. The use of multiple LOCI in DNA profiling significantly increases the power of discrimination and reduces the likelihood of a chance match between unrelated individuals. The comparison of STR profiles across multiple LOCIs provides an extremely high level of certainty in identifying individuals. As more LOCI are analyzed, the probability of two unrelated individuals having identical profiles becomes vanishingly small. This high degree of specificity is what makes STR profiling so powerful in forensic applications, allowing for confident identifications and definitive links between individuals and crime scenes even in complex cases.

Dr. Howard Baum played a pivotal role in the development of forensic DNA analysis in New York City. He started the Office of the Chief Medical Examiner's (OCME) Forensic Biology DNA Laboratory in 1990, building it from the ground up. Under his leadership, the laboratory grew from a small team of just a few scientists to a large, sophisticated operation with over 150 personnel, reflecting the increasing importance of DNA analysis in forensic investigations over the past three decades.

Beginning in 1998, Dr. Baum pioneered targeted male DNA testing on the male Y chromosome using Y-STR analysis. This innovation represented a significant advancement in forensic DNA technology for cases involving sexual assault or other scenarios where male DNA might be present in small quantities among samples heavily dominated by female genetic material, allowing for the detection and analysis of male DNA.

Selectively amplifying the short tandem repeats in regions on the Y-STR locus, using PCR, Polymerase Chain Reaction, enables a male profile to be determined. This technique involves targeting specific regions of the Y chromosome known to contain highly variable short tandem repeats. By amplifying these regions, forensic scientists can create a genetic profile unique to male individuals. The use of PCR is essential in this process, as it allows for the amplification of small amounts of DNA, making it possible to obtain usable profiles from limited samples.

Male profiles are easily differentiated from female profiles because they are generally shorter in length following amplification. This characteristic is due to the nature of Y-STR markers, which are found only on the Y chromosome, distinct from autosomal STR profiles. Y-STR analysis is extremely useful in cases where traditional methods of DNA analysis are impeded by the presence of a mixed male and female DNA sample. The development and implementation of Y-STR analysis under Dr. Baum's leadership has enhanced the capabilities of forensic laboratories worldwide, providing investigators with a powerful tool to isolate and analyze male DNA, enabling the identification of perpetrators in cases that might otherwise have remained unsolved.

When I first reached out to Jane Doe by phone notifying her that her cold case was being reopened, she burst into tears because she had a premonition the night before that a call would be coming. "I can't believe that you're calling me," she exclaimed. Even years after her assault, her visceral emotional response reflected the profound impact that unresolved cases can have on victims. The deep-seated hope for resolution underscores the vital importance of law enforcement's continued efforts to solve cold cases. These efforts serve not only to balance the scales of justice but also to provide a psychological floor for the emotional healing and well-being of survivors.

With a desire to restore her sense of faith, I approached our first conversation with sensitivity, stating that Deputy Chief Michael Osgood was an advocate. Despite her negative experiences with the NYPD in the past, I hoped to repair and curry trust with Jane by assuring her that she had the support from the highest levels of the NYPD's current leadership. Jane seemed to be grateful that we were once again looking into her case. Her gratitude despite grave disappointments in the past held the promise that rebuilding some semblance of trust with the law enforcement was within reach. After all she had gone through with the NYPD and the press, her reaction could have been, justifiably, very different.

In the years since her assault, Jane had retreated into relative anonymity in the time after her harrowing experience of becoming a victim of rape, the media debacle that ensued, and her libel suit against Mike McAlary and the *Daily News*. Given the opportunity to reclaim her privacy and to distance herself from the traumatic events and the public scrutiny that had dominated her life was essential to rebuilding her sense of self. The unforgiving glare of the media scrutiny had no doubt been traumatic illustrating the complex and often prolonged aftermath of sexual assault cases that gain public attention.

Perhaps reopening her cold case reignited a sense of agency that felt in some ways redemptive. The opportunity to assert her agency in the face of past victimization after many years of suspended action may have provided Jane with a renewed sense of purpose and control over her narrative. There was the potential to reflect anew on the refracted reality of those parts of herself that had shattered on the day of the assault and the subsequent news frenzy. This moment not only represented a potential breakthrough in her case but also a validation of all she'd endured in the years since.

Jane Doe agreed to meet me in person at the Midtown South Detective Squad to provide a buccal swab on November 22, 2017. The buccal swab collected cells from the inside of her cheeks and under the tongue; it's a standard and noninvasive method of obtaining DNA samples for forensic analysis. The swab collected a fresh sample of epithelial cells, which are rich in DNA and provide an excellent source for creating a reference profile. The epithelial cells which line the inside of the mouth are constantly shedding and regenerating, making them an ideal source of fresh genetic material. These cells contain nuclei with complete copies of an individual's DNA, allowing for the creation of a comprehensive genetic profile.

Jane's willingness to contribute a new sample, providing fresh DNA matter for comparison, was essential to obtaining a male profile, and, ultimately, to solving her case, albeit years after it should have been solved. Her sample was immediately vouchered and sent to the lab, maintaining the integrity of DNA evidence and the urgency of the investigation. Strict adherence to chain of custody procedures minimized any risks of contamination.

Over the next four weeks, a team of thirteen criminalists through the OCME Department of Forensic Biology DNA Laboratory worked on developing a male donor profile. This intensive effort by a large team of specialists ensured a comprehensive and meticulous examination of the evidence. A twenty-two LOCI CODIS-eligible profile was successfully obtained from the running shorts twenty-three years after the date of the crime, indicating the DNA found on this piece of clothing was highly stable. Obtaining a CODIS-eligible profile after such a long period was remarkable; the twenty-two LOCI profiles provided a high level of discrimination, significantly increasing the chances of a definitive match.

The profile was uploaded to SDIS, the State DNA Index System, on Wednesday, December 6, 2017, and just over two weeks later, on Wednesday, December 21st, a conclusive and definitive match was made to convicted Offender James Edward Webb, New York State ID #01206434K, from the DNA which was uploaded to CODIS seventeen years earlier in July of 2000. The fact that Webb's DNA had been in the system for seventeen years before matching the isolated male sample derived from Jane Doe's running shorts perfectly illustrated the power of DNA databases in solving cold cases years and decades after the initial crime.

Chapter 8

THE CRIMINAL HISTORY OF A CAREER RAPIST

One week after I'd obtained a positive ID on Jane Doe's rapist, I made a trip to Sing Sing Correctional Facility, a maximum-security prison in Ossining, New York, 30 miles outside the city, to speak with him. This correctional facility, which houses New York's most dangerous male offenders, has a long and notorious history dating back to 1826 and remains one of the oldest penal institutions in the United States. Sing Sing's imposing structure, situated along the east bank of the Hudson River, is home to some of the most infamous criminals in American history and has become synonymous with harsh incarceration in popular culture.

As I approached the prison, the stark contrast between the beautiful river views and the confining walls of the institution was not lost on me. The knowledge that I was about to confront a convicted serial rapist within these walls added a dimension of leaden gravity to the encounter. James Webb is not eligible for parole until December 3, 2070, which means he will live out the rest of his natural life behind bars.

In the time after he attacked Jane Doe in April of 1994, he was sentenced and incarcerated in 1997 with an aggregate sentence of seventy-five years to life for four other completed rapes, targeting women ages sixteen to thirty-seven from August 17, 1995, to December 4, 1995. Committing multiple serious offenses in rapid succession over a short period, his predatory nature and appetite for violence seemed indiscriminate, making him a significant threat to public safety, a seeming justification for the harsh sentence he received. His actions not only devastated the lives of his direct victims but also sent shockwaves through the communities where these crimes occurred.

Before Sing Sing, he was an inmate at Sullivan Correctional Facility, also a maximum-security prison, in Fallsburg, in Sullivan County, New York. The specifics as to what prompted the transfer are unknown, but the reason may have been logistics. Sing Sing's proximity to New York City, just thirty miles north rather than one hundred miles northwest of the city, would make visits to Webb more accessible for legal representatives or family members. His transfer from one supermax to another confirms his status as an inmate who requires stringent containment measures. Sullivan Correctional Facility, like Sing Sing, is known for housing some of New York's most dangerous offenders who have been convicted of the most serious crimes.

If Webb had been identified as Jane Doe's rapist in the first year her case was actively investigated from April of 1994 to January of 1995, perhaps Webb would have been incarcerated, or at least held securely on remand, and unable to carry out his subsequent attacks. The delay in identifying Webb as Jane Doe's attacker allowed him to remain at large, during which time he committed multiple other serious offenses against women. The potential to prevent future crimes by apprehending offenders quickly is a compelling argument for prioritizing sexual assault investigations and allocating sufficient resources to them. Prioritizing sexual assault investigations involves rapid processing of forensic evidence, adequate staffing of specialized units, ongoing training for investigators, improved coordination between agencies, and implementation of victim-centered approaches.

As a serial rapist, Webb may have victimized more than the four women he was convicted of raping, a possibility given that sex crimes are widely underreported. Of the known attacks on five women of varying ages, one had managed to flee after wresting her way out of his grip before a forcible rape took place. The true extent of his crimes as a serial rape offender was likely greater than what is officially documented. As measuring recidivism rates is an inexact science, one study found that rapists had a sexual recidivism rate of 14 percent after five years and 24 percent after fifteen years and an even higher percentage after twenty-five years. Webb's lengthy sentence, making him ineligible for parole until 2070, effectively prevents the prospect of any further victimization as rapists usually do not prey on victims while incarcerated. For Webb, whose victims were female, the single-sex population of male inmates at Sing Sing further diminishes the prospect of him committing sex crimes while behind bars. Beyond keeping Webb imprisoned, an examination exploring the root causes of sexual violence is likely needed to understand the psychological drives that breed violence in someone who commits sex crimes serially. This type of research would be effective in developing prevention strategies, treatment programs, and risk assessment tools. Understanding the factors that contribute to serial sexual offending can inform both criminal justice policies and public health initiatives aimed at reducing sexual violence in society.

Sitting across from Webb, who had waived his Miranda rights in an indication he may have been willing to discuss his criminal past, I did a reverse identification by showing him a picture of Jane Doe. Presenting a photo of the victim to an offender is a common investigative technique used to gauge a perpetrator's reaction and potentially elicit a confession or other valuable information. Webb's subsequent denial frustrated me.

He said, "This is the first time that I've seen this woman. I never had sex with this woman. I don't even know her. I don't know what you're talking about." Webb's categorical denial, while not entirely unexpected, left me somewhat disappointed though his like didn't strike me as a bald-faced deception. The vehemence and claim of never having seen Jane Doe before, coupled with the assertion that he had never had sexual contact with her, seemed designed to distance himself completely from any association with the crime he's committed. My career as a detective has given me plenty of experience with reading suspects and convicted offenders. Years of interviewing while navigating complex investigations had honed my ability to interpret nuanced verbal and nonverbal cues of those involved in criminal cases, helping me to discern both deception and truthfulness. What I was witnessing seemed more like self-delusion and total lack of remorse for the pain he'd caused by his terrifying actions, common traits among repeat violent offenders.

At the time of his sentencing, his actions had resulted in multiple counts of indictment for rape, sodomy, arson, and robbery. The breadth and severity of these charges paint a picture of a prolific and versatile offender, whose criminal behavior spanned a range of serious offenses. His record of escalating criminal behavior for both sexual and nonsexual crimes, offenses executed with an utter disregard for social norms and presiding laws, buttresses the argument that he is a threat to society. Though Webb would never again be a free man, engaging him face-to-face within these prison walls, he was still far from owning up to the violence he'd subjected his victims to.

This reluctance or inability to acknowledge the full extent of his crimes is not uncommon among long-term offenders, particularly those convicted of violent crimes. Perhaps this may be attributed to the specific psychological make-up of violent offenders and others within the prison system who seem to be beyond the hope of rehabilitation. Webb's refusal to take responsibility for his actions, despite the overwhelming evidence and his conviction, could also be attributed to some form of cognitive dissonance. A psychological defense mechanism could be in place to protect his self-image and to allow himself to avoid confronting the full weight of his actions and their consequences.

After I mentioned to Webb that his DNA sample, which was collected in the time after he was incarcerated and then uploaded to the Convicted Offender Index, matched the male profile from the forensic evidence obtained at the scene of his crimes, he balked and revised his response by stating, "Well, I didn't rape those women. I only robbed them." This sudden change in Webb's narrative is a common occurrence when confronted with DNA evidence, as it often forces suspects to adjust their stories to account for the new information. The shift from complete denial to partial admission is a telling moment in the interview process, revealing the suspect's attempt to minimize their culpability or negotiate their perceived level of guilt.

For those inmates serving lengthy sentences, the refusal to admit guilt can stem from various factors, psychological or otherwise, including using denial as a coping mechanism developed over years of incarceration, or a misguided attempt to maintain a semblance of control. Denial can serve as a psychological shield and can be seen as a response to the loss of autonomy that comes with long-term incarceration.

There are any number of reasons from compulsive lying to underlying mental health issues as to why Webb would make the claim, "I didn't rape these women," though he'd already been convicted. Compulsive lying, for instance, might have been a long-standing behavioral pattern for Webb, possibly stemming from a personality disorder.

In some cases of clinically compulsive lying, an individual may come to believe his or her own fabrications, blurring the line between reality and fiction in their own mind.

Underlying mental health issues could also play a significant role in Webb's contradictory statements. Deeply entrenched patterns of antisocial behavior consistent with antisocial personality disorder, narcissistic personality disorder, or even certain types of psychosis could contribute to a distorted perception of reality or an inability to accept responsibility for one's actions. These conditions can affect an individual's perception of reality, their sense of empathy, or their ability to take responsibility for their actions. In some cases, long-term incarceration itself can exacerbate mental health problems, affecting an inmate's ability to process and discuss their past actions rationally. Moreover, Webb's revised claim of "only" robbing the women could be seen as an attempt at cognitive dissonance reduction. By admitting to a lesser crime while denying the more severe offense of rape, he might have been attempting to manipulate my perception of him.

I asked him to memorialize his response to me with a signed handwritten note, which he completed. Obtaining a written statement is a standard investigative practice that provides a tangible record of Webb's admissions, though he was not any more forthcoming in his written account than what he was willing to disclose verbally. His limited disclosure could have been a deliberate strategy to reveal as little information as possible while still appearing to comply. While Webb's written statement did not provide any new insights, it became a part of the overall investigative record.

Webb was born in 1950 and had spent a significant portion of his adult life incarcerated. Born in the mid-twentieth century, Webb came of age during a time of significant social and cultural change in America, yet his life trajectory was marked by repeated criminal behavior in defiance of adapting to societal norms. His long history within the criminal justice system points to a pattern of criminal behavior and a series of serious offenses that began early in his adulthood indicating the failure of early intervention or rehabilitation efforts to interrupt a lifestyle of deeply ingrained predilections to engage in criminal activity.

Upon his release following a twenty-year prison term in 1993, for which he served the entire sentence, he committed forcible rape in 1994 in attacking Jane Doe in Prospect Park. Reoffending less than a year after his release as a parolee highlights the challenges of rehabilitation and the potential dangers of releasing long-term offenders without adequate support or supervision. Webb's actions demonstrate a failure of the correctional system to effectively address his criminal tendencies suggesting that the two long decades Webb spent in prison did very little to address his propensity for violence or to prepare him for successful reintegration into society. Webb's return to violent crime is a case in point about the effectiveness of parole systems, the availability and quality of post-release support services, and the overall approach to prisoner reentry. It also points to the difficulties in predicting and preventing recidivism in violent offenders.

The impact of Webb's crimes extends far beyond the immediate physical harm to his victims who've endured a ripple effect of untold misery, stress, depression, and terror as a result of his violent crimes. The psychological trauma inflicted on those he attacked, as well as their families and communities, can last for years or even generations, fundamentally altering his victims' sense of safety and ability to trust. This trauma extends beyond the individual victim to affect their family and friends who may experience secondary trauma, while grappling with feelings of guilt, anger, and helplessness in trying to support their loved one.

The drain on tax dollars for the state of New York to prosecute the defendant's rape case is considerable with direct costs of investigation, prosecution, and incarceration as well as indirect costs associated with increased demand for mental health services and victim support programs, for example. The cost of human suffering and the economic impact extends to the victims themselves, many of whom face substantial medical bills, therapy costs, and potential loss of income due to the psychological aftermath of the assault. The true cost, however, lies in their dreams deferred, the relationships strained or broken, and the unfulfilled potential as victims struggle to rebuild their lives in the wake of such traumatic experiences.

Many pattern offenders like Webb believe that they are smarter than the law and can evade being caught. A common psychological trait among serial offenders, often rooted in a combination of narcissism, overconfidence, and a distorted perception of their own abilities is in play. Overconfidence, fueled by successful evasion of capture, can lead to increasingly risky behavior and a false sense of invincibility. The distorted perception of their own abilities may cause offenders to believe they have outsmarted the system, when in reality, their crimes may simply have gone undetected or unconnected for a period of time. Narcissism is often coupled with a lack of empathy, allowing offenders to rationalize or dismiss the harm they cause to others. They can be prone to an exaggerated sense of self-importance and a belief in one's own exceptional abilities, leading to increasingly risky behavior and a tendency to underestimate law enforcement capabilities, especially if they have successfully evaded capture for some time.

Whether this was Webb's mindset or not, the language that he used to threaten his female victims into submission while brandishing a knife, or a screwdriver, established a modus operandi (MO), as he said and used the same words telling each of his victims, "Shut up or I'll kill you." The use of a direct, concise threat suggests a desire for immediate compliance and a way to instill fear in his victims quickly. Establishing a ritualized pattern of behavior is invaluable to investigators in linking multiple crimes to a single perpetrator. Studying the repetition of specific phrases and actions across different attacks can serve as a set of clues helping law enforcement to develop a profile and build a case against a serial offender. These behavioral consistencies can be just as important as physical evidence in establishing a pattern of criminal activity, as recognizing these patterns can lead to breakthroughs in cold cases.

Webb raped women in public parks, school yards, and abandoned buildings,[1] opportunistic settings where potential victims, targeting strangers rather than acquaintances, could be found alone or vulnerable. Public parks and school yards are areas where people often feel a false sense of security, especially during daylight hours, making them ideal hunting grounds for predators like Webb. These locations also typically offer a mix of open spaces and secluded areas, allowing an attacker to quickly transition from a public setting to a more private one.

His committing crimes in public spaces demonstrated both a bold audacity and an appetite for risk-taking behavior that suggests a thrill-seeking aspect, as if he were thumbing his nose at law enforcement and potential witnesses. The attack in an abandoned building suggests that Webb may have scouted the location in advance. This level of preparation indicates a more calculated approach to some of his crimes, while others appear to have been more opportunistic. Prospect Park, where he attacked Jane Doe, was a public space with entry and exit routes that he was likely familiar with. While it's a common trait among serial offenders to choose to operate in areas they know well, Webb's choice of Prospect Park, as an attack site, speaks to either his sense of invulnerability or a sense of apathy, caring little about whether he got caught.

Webb has a long history of violence against women with his first recorded sex crime of Rape 1 going back to February of 1968. This early onset of serious sexual offenses indicates a pattern of criminal behavior that began in his late teens or early twenties. Research has proven that offenders who dabble in petty larceny and other criminal activities at a young age are more likely to persist in criminal behavior that escalates throughout their lives. The severity of the charge, Rape 1, highlighted the violent nature of Webb's crimes from the outset.

After a robbery Webb committed in September of 1968, he was sentenced to one year and did the time. The quick transition from sexual assault to property crime indicates a versatile criminal profile, which is often associated with higher rates of recidivism and a profile that is challenging to address through conventional methods of rehabilitation.

Then he was arrested again in November of 1969 on multiple charges of Rape 1, reckless endangerment, and possession of a firearm for which he was sentenced to five years and served a partial sentence. The recurrence of Rape 1 charges, coupled with additional violent offenses, demonstrated a clear pattern of escalating criminal behavior. The inclusion of firearms charges suggested an increased willingness to use or threaten deadly force in the commission of his crimes. The range of criminal activities, spanning from property crimes such as robbery to the far more egregious and personally invasive offense of sexual assault reflected Webb's heightened disregard for human dignity and a profound lack of empathy consistent with criminological research on individuals who choose to become career criminals.

Serial rapists are generally not offending while they are incarcerated, so recidivism by released inmates occurs at the next available opportunity to commit a sex crime. Following his release on March 7, 1973, Webb went on a rampage of criminal activity committing at least four sex crimes from April to October of 1973. This rapid succession of offenses within a short period demonstrates the intensity of his criminal predilections. This pattern of attacks on women back in the 1970s would parallel a future spree over two decades later in the 1990s from August to December of 1995. The recurrence of similar patterns of behavior across such a long time span is not only indicative of Webb's deeply ingrained criminal tendencies but also suggests an utter lack of deterrence despite previous punishments which draws into sharp focus the limitations of the criminal justice system in effectively rehabilitating repeat offenders even over long stretches of incarceration.

Webb went on crime sprees the moment he was released from jail in 1969 and 1973. His October 1993 release date stands out as an exception to his other release dates in that he seemed to have suspended his criminal activities for a six-month period until the rape of Jane Doe in April 1994. This brief period of compliant behavior may be attributed to Webb potentially having a meaningful support system, or employment that may have temporarily suppressed his criminal tendencies. Otherwise, Webb re-committed violent crimes immediately after his release from prison only to cause terror and havoc during his fleeting periods as a free man.

While doing time from 1973 onward, for the rape of six women, a conviction for possession of a dangerous weapon added another forty-two months to his sentence. This additional conviction for a weapons offense demonstrates Webb's continued involvement in criminal activities even while incarcerated. The possession of a dangerous weapon in prison suggests a propensity for violence and a disregard for institutional rules, further cementing Webb's status as a high-risk offender.

Webb was incarcerated for two decades from 1973 to 1993 for which he maxed out, completing his full prison term before being released on parole on October 15, 1993. This extended period of incarceration, spanning two decades, represents a significant portion of Webb's adult life spent behind bars. The fact that he served his full sentence without having been released any earlier indicates either a lack of participation in rehabilitation programs, poor behavior while incarcerated, or the severity of his crimes precluding early release considerations.

Following the quiet period through April of 1994 in which Webb was reporting to his parole officer consistently and going uncaught for the rape he'd committed in Prospect Pack in late April, come July of 1994 there's a sealed arrest record for a robbery. This initial period of apparent compliance with parole conditions, followed by the commission of the Prospect Park rape and a subsequent robbery, illustrates the challenges of monitoring and managing high-risk offenders in the community despite the supervision and potential support provided by the parole system.

Sometime afterward, he was also arrested for grand larceny in the third-degree which caused him to miss his check-in with his parole officer in February of 1995. For the larceny, and for violating the conditions of his parole, Webb was back behind bars for a six-month stint at Orleans Correctional Facility, a medium-security prison for males in NY state, from February to August. However, the brevity of this incarceration, given Webb's extensive criminal history, raises questions about the effectiveness of short-term re-imprisonment in deterring future criminal behavior for a chronic offender like himself with a history of violent crimes.

Upon his release on August 16, 1995, he wasted no time and committed Rape 1, Sodomy 1, and Robbery the following day on August 17th, marking the beginning of a series of violent attacks that would terrorize the Fort Greene neighborhood of Brooklyn through December. Three of his attacks were completed forcible rapes and sodomy, or attempted sodomy, in the 88th Precinct[2] in the Fort Greene neighborhood of Brooklyn, all within ten blocks of Lafayette and Marcy Avenue, where he shared a basement apartment with his elderly aunt and a niece. The concentration of these attacks within a small geographic area close to home is not uncommon among serial offenders, as it allows them to quickly retreat to a safe location after committing a crime. Webb did not discriminate based on age and was willing to target a minor who was just sixteen years old.

More likely to be recognized and caught by repeatedly committing crimes in the same area, it was the composite police sketch being circulated among law enforcement officers, which depicted a clean-shaven man with a gap in his front teeth, that ultimately led to his capture and arrest. The decision to continue offending in the same neighborhood despite the increased risk of recognition suggests either a lack of concern for being caught or an inability to control his criminal impulses.

The fact that Webb was living with family members while committing these crimes shows him maintaining a facade of normalcy in his home life while engaging in violent criminal behavior, a characteristic often seen in serial offenders who can compartmentalize their criminal activities from their day-to-day interactions with family and acquaintances.

While the police sketch that Jane Doe had provided back in April of 1994 was also a close resemblance to Webb's visage, portraying him with a mustache and beard wearing a black hat with a brim that sits low on his forehead, unfortunately, the original sketch failed to be a useful tool in solving her case. Despite the accuracy of Jane Doe's description, her sketch did not lead to Webb's identification or arrest at the time, underscoring the limitations of relying solely on evidence such as eyewitness descriptions.

Notably, James Webb's parole officers James Mack and William McCartney recognized the more recent sketch, with the clean-shaven portrait, as the likeness of one of their parolees and notified detectives working the serial rape cases that they believed Webb was a suspect. The interagency communication proved to be very valuable as the ongoing supervision of parole was key to identifying the perpetrator in the most recent rash of crimes.

A specific physical characteristic, the detail of a gap in his front teeth, was instrumental to informing his identity. Such distinctive features often play a significant role in eyewitness identifications and can be key elements in linking suspects to crimes. Staging a strategic arrest, Webb was taken into custody on December 6, 1995, when he next reported to his parole officers. Two days earlier, on December 4th, he'd committed Rape 1, Sodomy 1, Robbery 3, and Arson in the 71st Precinct. Following the sexual assault, Webb was unable to find his wallet, and he threatened to burn the place down, which he was successful in doing. This level of impulsivity was a glimpse into his willingness to resort to extreme behavior.

Coordinating his arrest with when he was expected to check in with his parole officer was a thought-out tactical approach by law enforcement to apprehend him in a controlled environment. This strategy minimized the risk of flight or potential harm to the others during the arrest process. The interagency cooperation between Webb's parole officers and detectives made it possible to apprehend a dangerous offender.

Post-arrest, a direct comparison of Webb's DNA to the DNA of the secretions of semen he left in at least three of his victims' bodies, confirmed the two DNA profiles were a match, definitively linking him to multiple crimes and his pattern of serial offenses. Thereafter his victims identified him in a police lineup and he was charged. With the corroboration of the victim's accounts, there was plenty of evidence to support the charges and to build a solid case against him. The combination of evidence DNA, eyewitness testimony, and physical evidence created a comprehensive picture of Webb's criminal activities, making it difficult for the defense to challenge the prosecution's case.

Facing four counts of rape, Webb pleaded not guilty, and when the case went to trial, Webb's defense attorney filed a motion to prevent the defendant's lengthy prior criminal history, and the fact that Webb had been released from jail less than three days before the first of these serial assaults, from being admissible as evidence. This is a common legal tactic in criminal defense strategy, known as a motion in limine, which safeguards the defendant's constitutional right to a fair trial as guaranteed by the Sixth Amendment, by preventing potentially prejudicial information from influencing the jury's decision-making process.

As jurors might be more inclined to assume guilt based on past actions rather than the evidence presented for the current case, a defendant is judged solely on the evidence related to the current charges, rather than on their past behavior or criminal record. If the sensitive information of Webb being an inmate who was released from jail just days before the first alleged assault for which he was being tried were presented to the jury, it could create a narrative of immediate recidivism that might be difficult for the defense to overcome. The defense's motion to exclude this information demonstrates an understanding of the potential impact such details could have on the jury's perception. By attempting to keep this information out of the trial, the defense aims to ensure that Webb is judged solely on the merits of the current case, without the shadow of his past influencing the jury's decision. As the presumption of innocence is the cornerstone of our criminal justice system, any admissible evidence must be directly relevant to the allegations and charges at hand. This aims to maintain the integrity of the judicial process and is a critical safeguard against wrongful convictions. While such motions are common in criminal proceedings, they are not unilaterally guaranteed by the judge, who ultimately is the one to decide the potential prejudice against the probative value of the evidence.

Webb's defense attorneys also prevented the police sketch that was instrumental in obtaining his arrest, and the mention of Webb being identified by a victim as wearing standard-issue white athletics shoes, which are routinely given to newly released prison inmates, from becoming admissible evidence.[3] While sketches can be crucial investigative tools, their use in court can be challenged on various grounds. Police sketches are often created based on witness descriptions and can be subject to inaccuracies due to factors such as the witness's memory, the stress experienced by the witness during the crime, the subjective skill of the sketch artist, and potential unconscious biases in the creation process. Defense attorneys frequently argue that such sketches are unreliable and potentially prejudicial, as they may lead jurors to make assumptions about the defendant's guilt based on a potentially flawed representation.

The decision to exclude any mention in the court proceeding of Webb wearing standard-issue white athletic shoes was another significant victory for the defense. The admission of this evidence could have been particularly damning as it would likely have suggested to the jury that Webb had recently been released from prison, potentially biasing the jury against him. By preventing this information from being presented in court, Webb's attorneys were able to maintain a focus on the current charges without the shadow of his past incarceration influencing the jury's perception. Such information might influence jurors to make assumptions about Webb's character rather than focusing on the specific allegations and evidence related to the current charges. By challenging the admissibility of certain evidence, Webb's defense team played a crucial role in upholding the principles of due process and the defendant's right to be presumed innocent until proven guilty beyond a reasonable doubt.

A physical exam, ordered by the prosecutor in the time after he was arrested, confirmed that Webb was sterile due to congenital bilateral undescended testicles, an inherited condition that is fairly rare in the general population. This medical condition, known as cryptorchidism when bilateral impacts fertility, is typically diagnosed and treated in early childhood. The rarity of this condition in adults, combined with its direct relevance to the forensic evidence in sexual assault cases, was especially noteworthy in Webb's cases as this unique characteristic was confirmed by the semen samples collected from the crime scenes, which contained seminal fluid but no spermatozoa. The statistical infrequency of bilateral cryptorchidism in the adult male population significantly narrowed the pool of potential suspects. This medical condition essentially served as a biological signature, of sorts, linking Webb to the crimes in a way that was both highly specific and scientifically verifiable.

Why this finding did not intuitively lead to Jane Doe's case being reinvestigated sooner is perplexing, as the absence of spermatozoa which indicated the secretor's prostate could not manufacture sperm was well documented in Det. Sorrentino's DD5, the Detective Division Form 5. Even though Webb's defense team was successful in shaping the narrative presented to the jury by blocking prosecutors' attempts to enter Webb's inherited medical condition as evidence, the DNA forensic evidence presented for the jury in the trial would prove to be equally damning and irrefutable. The accuracy of DNA analysis, which has become the gold standard for identification in recent years, while not infallible, has been upheld by the forensic community as nearly irrefutable and often supersedes other forms of admissible evidence. While the judicial outcome of a case should not rely solely on DNA evidence, corroborated with other forms of evidence, the power of DNA analysis in providing conclusive identification is undeniable.

The apparent disconnect between Webb's documented sterility and the physical forensic evidence from Jane Doe's case shows an organizational deficit in how key findings were poorly cross-referenced across separate criminal investigations which end up being related. It raises questions about the protocols in place for re-examining cold cases when new information comes to light. If there had been adequate protocols in place, it's feasible that Jane Doe's attacker would have been identified at the same time as the cases of the four victims who followed, saving the survivor a lifetime of unresolved trauma.

After the prosecution had forty witnesses take the stand to testify, compared to the defense who only called on three witnesses,[4] a jury found James Edward Webb guilty on October 29, 1997. The large disparity in the number of witnesses called by each side likely had an impact on the jury's perception of the case. The prosecution's ability to present such a large number of witnesses may have allowed them to build a more compelling narrative of Webb's guilt compared to the defense's case for his innocence.

Justice Abraham G. Gerges of the Kings County Supreme Court,[5] in Brooklyn, sentenced James Webb later that year on December 23rd to concurrent terms of twenty-years to life in prison,[6] requiring him to serve a minimum term of seventy-five years before becoming eligible for parole—a day that he will never come to see. This exceptionally long sentence and consecutive terms, rather than concurrent ones, suggests that the judge aimed to ensure Webb would remain incarcerated for the rest of his natural life. Webb will never have the opportunity to terrorize a neighborhood or claim another rape victim outside of a prison cell ever again. The outcome of Webb's trial and sentencing represented a significant victory for law enforcement and the prosecution. Cases involving repeat offenders like this one often spark discussions about the effectiveness of rehabilitation programs and the role of parole in the criminal justice system.

One of the major reasons parole boards grant parole is as a mechanism for gradual reentry into the community for inmates who have a minimized risk and likelihood of offending. However, for an inmate such as James Webb, with an established pattern of recidivism, because the likelihood of his reoffending is a foregone conclusion, he received one of the most severe punishments imposed by the criminal justice system. His long sentence of incarceration effectively removed the possibility of parole during his natural life and prioritized public safety over the potential for individual rehabilitation.

And though Jane Doe's perpetrator was now captured and being held to account, never to commit another sex crime again, Jane would have to wait another two decades, and what seems like an interminable amount of time, before receiving any such confirmation. This prolonged period of uncertainty and lack of closure can create a perpetual sense of vulnerability and significantly impact a victim's ability to move forward, as the constant fear of a perpetrator at large can persist for years.

In the immediate aftermath of her physical attack, Jane faced an excoriating assault on her integrity in being disbelieved, and without any resolution in her case, she was left with the task of having to move forward with her life, while coping with the long-term ramifications that all trauma survivors bear. This dual trauma—the physical attack and the subsequent accusations of disbelief from others—was a heavy cross to hear resulting in ongoing emotional and psychological duress. The multifaceted detrimental impact of such a prolonged period without resolution cannot be overstated. This extended timeframe between the crime and the resolution highlights a significant issue in the criminal justice system—the often slow pace at which cases are resolved and the limited communication with victims about the status of their cases exacerbate feelings of powerlessness.

Rebuilding her life after a violent crime involved not only processing the trauma over many years but also reconstructing her sense of personal safety and learning how to trust others again. Survivors often require professional help, a strong support system, and an immense amount of personal fortitude in the face of such adversity. Trauma-informed therapists can provide survivors like Jane Doe with coping strategies and tools to process their experiences. Recovery from trauma is rarely a linear process and the path to healing involves setbacks and ongoing struggles, but the courageous act of rebuilding one's life day by day serves as a testament to the human spirit's capacity for resilience.

In February of 1997, ten months before James Edward Webb's sentencing by Justice Gerges, the lawsuit in which Attorney Garbus represented Jane Doe as the plaintiff in her libel suit against columnist Mike McAlary and the *New York Daily News* was dismissed on a pretrial motion. Judge Charles E. Ramos had ruled in favor of McAlary's First Amendment protections. The dismissal, occurring just months before Webb's criminal sentencing, creates a stark contrast between the outcomes of the criminal and civil proceedings related to Jane Doe's case, underscoring the different legal standards and considerations at play in criminal versus civil proceedings.

In a cruel twist of fate, Jane Doe was not privy to information that could have provided her with enormous consolation and relief had she known that James Webb, the man who'd attacked her, was sentenced in October of 1997 to live out the rest of his natural life behind bars. While the criminal justice system shackled Webb, holding him accountable for breaking the law, the civil court system determined that McAlary's published columns were protected under the First Amendment, regardless of their impact on Jane Doe.

Chapter 9

LONG-AWAITED APOLOGIES

"I *knew* this day would come! Thank you for believing in me! Thank you. I knew *one day*, this day would come."

These were Jane Doe's words to me, poignant in their gratitude. After sending detectives and a supervisor to her residence in my stead, I called her to deliver the good news. We had successfully identified the man who had attacked her over twenty-three years ago. The relief and emotion in her voice were palpable, a testament to the weight she had carried for more than two decades. Jane Doe was finally able to put a name to the perpetrator who had so profoundly impacted her life. It was one of my proudest moments as an NYPD detective, a culmination of years of dedicated work and perseverance.

The Special Victims DNA Cold Case Squad was created precisely for moments like these—to provide some measure of closure for survivors of heinous crimes who may have long given up hope of justice, or survivors who had held onto unwavering hope in the face of what must have seemed like insurmountable odds. By dedicating resources and expertise specifically to cold case sexual assaults, this specialized unit demonstrated a commitment to pursuing justice regardless of the passage of time, recognizing the importance of resolving these cases, even years after the fact.

For Jane Doe, and countless others like her, this identification represented a validation of her experience and a chance to reclaim a part of herself that she may have felt had been stolen from her. The identification of her perpetrator, even decades later, was a pivotal moment that brought her healing as a survivor full circle. For the broader community of survivors, each solved cold case sends a powerful message that their experiences matter and that law enforcement remains committed to seeking justice on their behalf. The work of the Special Victims DNA Cold Case Squad also serves as a deterrent to potential offenders, demonstrating that ongoing advancements in forensic technology backed by dedicated investigative efforts will continue to expand the possibilities for solving cold cases even decades after a crime has been committed.

A mature woman in her fifties, Jane could finally unburden herself of the uncertainty that was likely a constant and haunting companion in the time since her rape. I hoped this watershed moment would change her future for the better, ushering in a newfound emotional security of knowing that the risk of future predation by Webb had dropped to zero. He would never sexually violate another woman ever again. While the trauma of Jane Doe's experience could never be erased, knowing the identity of her attacker and that he was no longer a threat may have allowed Jane to move forward with her life in ways that were previously impossible.

While her vindication stopped short of being able to pursue prosecution, as the statute of limitations of five years for a sex crime from 1994 had already passed, formal apologies from the New York Police Department were forthcoming. The apologies represented an important acknowledgment of the mishandling of Jane's case and the additional trauma she endured as a result. This resolution, while not providing the full justice that the prosecution might have offered, still marked a significant milestone in Jane's journey. It demonstrated the importance of continued efforts in solving cold cases and the potential for DNA evidence to provide answers long after traditional investigative methods have been exhausted.

Robert Boyce, who was Chief of Detectives in 2017 said, "You can imagine how emotional she was. She cried last night when we told her we had the guy. I think my detectives cried with her."[1] Boyce's words provide a glimpse into the emotional impact of solving a cold case, for everyone involved showing that officers are just as deeply invested in the cases they work on and the outcomes achieved. Mincing no words, Boyce said, "He's a savage,"[2] referring to James Webb. This blunt characterization by the chief of detectives reflects the revulsion that even a seasoned law enforcement officer can have toward perpetrators of such heinous acts.

Jane Doe's attorney Martin Garbus, said, "She has lived for twenty-three years with the allegation that she was not telling the truth. The press misreported the story, only adding an additional level of pain."[3] Garbus's critique makes plain the terrible ordeal Jane experienced as a secondary victimization when she was disbelieved and when her story was misrepresented.

Shortly after the case was solved, Jane Doe's personal statement about her long-suffering tribulations, and her request for apologies from John Miller, the Deputy Commissioner of Public Information for the NYPD in 1994, the NYPD, and the *Daily News*, were featured in *The New York Times* on January 18, 2018:

> John Miller, I'm a person, just like the woman you were born from. You owe me an apology. NYPD, I'm a person, just like the rest of the taxpayers whom you exist to serve. You owe me an apology. *Daily News*, I am a person, whom you printed egregiously cruel lies about, without any real evidence. Those lies shattered what was left of my not-quite 26-year-old psyche. You owe me an apology.[4]

This statement from Jane Doe encapsulates the profound impact that the mishandling of her case and subsequent media coverage had on her life. Her words highlight the dehumanizing effect of being doubted, misrepresented, and publicly maligned in the aftermath of a traumatic assault. By emphasizing her personhood in each request for an apology, Jane Doe poignantly reminds those involved of the human cost of their actions and decisions.

John Miller, who was the Deputy Commissioner of Intelligence & Counterterrorism of the NYPD in 2018 before he retired from the force in 2022, offered words of apology hours later for passing on speculative information, which was reported by McAlary in his *Daily News* columns as an embellishment of erroneous fact. Precisely because Miller was to deceased *Daily News* columnist Mike McAlary the "catch basin"[5] for information on all police matters, Miller apologized to Jane Doe for falling short of fulfilling "a higher obligation to the citizens we serve, especially the witnesses to and victims of crimes." He acknowledged that how he chose to deploy the misinformation, perhaps overly fast and loose for NYPD cases under active investigation, "revictimized a person who was already the victim of a terrible crime."[6]

"To see in print that police sources had called me a liar had a silencing effect on me, to say the least." She added, "I paid a terrible, terrible price for my #MeToo," referring to the movement that has generated public dialogue for the creation of systemic reforms that better hold to account perpetrators of sexual harassment and assault. The hashtag, utilized in the rapid-fire transmission of ideas on social media platforms, was an effective way to raise visibility around the widespread prevalence of sexual harassment and assault.

While Jane Doe was never named in McAlary's columns, and instead identified by age, race, and sexual orientation, it was the accusation behind his story and his tenacious grip over the claim that the rape was a hoax that did so much harm. In her January 2018 statement to *The New York Times*, Jane Doe, who was now a mother, chose to recontextualize her firsthand experience with trauma by advocating for a systemic change in how sexual assault, and its victims, are viewed in the culture writ large:

> Today larger societal issues are framing my personal experience of trauma, just as they did then. There are thousands of cold cases, thousands more rape kits from the 1990s and beyond that have not been tested with modern technology. Don't those victims deserve closure, too? There are still victims receiving substandard treatment from cops and ER doctors who don't know how to deal with assault victims sensitively. Can't we put training in place to correct that? Most disturbingly, stories of assault are still discounted; cases are not vigorously prosecuted. Schools and workplaces deal with sexual assaults as internal disciplinary matters instead of as what they are—crimes.[7]

Police Commissioner James P. O'Neill delivered a personal apology to Jane Doe, and published a public apology through the official website of the City of New York, nyc.gov, on October 28, 2018.

> To the survivor: As Police Commissioner, I extend my heartfelt apology for all aspersions cast upon your credibility by NYPD personnel those many years ago. And I apologize for the NYPD's role

> in the quarter-century of questions that so wrongly surrounded your case. We know the damage that sexual assaults inflict on survivors. Compounding that damage with insensitive comments and wild conspiracy theories only further amplifies the cruelty and injustice of the initial crime itself. For that, I am deeply and profoundly sorry.[8]

He went on to acknowledge how advances in forensic DNA analysis were key to solving Jane Doe's case, "I am grateful, too, for the improved forensic technology that, in the intervening years, has now allowed us to affirm—at long last, and beyond the shadow of a doubt—that the Prospect Park survivor absolutely told the truth."

Jane Doe, in having received the Commissioner's apology commented, "I wanted to see this happen so that the N.Y.P.D. would have to take a public stance in support of survivors, so that there would be a public statement that would make it clear that it was safe and beneficial for survivors to come forward to the police, and that they would not be attacked or pilloried by the police."[9]

Attorney Martin Garbus praised O'Neill's written apology as remarkable but held the reservation, "It's unfortunate that it didn't go further and highlight the people in the police department that allowed this to happen." Indeed, there is no mention of John Miller in O'Neill's apology. Garbus adds, "You really have to show who the people were who did it. It's not enough to say the institution did it. You have to highlight the people who did it."[10]

Garbus risked his reputation and career as a foremost First Amendment attorney to take on a libel suit in which the plaintiff, whom he represented, was suing a member of the press and his employer, the media organization. As a consequence, Garbus's firm was temporarily suspended from a prominent trade organization called the Libel Defense Resource Center, or LDRC, because Garbus was acting against the grain of its ideological bylaws, in spirit if not in letter. A part of LDRC's mission is to defend the freedom of expression for journalists and media organizations facing libel and defamation litigation. Garbus went out on a limb in launching a bid to bring a gross abuse of that freedom to the fore.

As a further consequence, Garbus's law firm lost a major media client and other clients cut ties as well in short order, highlighting the far-reaching implications of high-profile cases and public controversies.

To rectify the losses due to such a harsh reprimand, Garbus met with his partners and offered to resign,[11] attesting to his willingness to prioritize the firm's interests over his own position. Though John Miller had finally given Jane Doe her long-awaited apology, soon after her case was solved, Martin Garbus believes Miller should have resigned from his post with the NYPD. While the apology was important and necessary, it didn't redress the magnitude of his mistake and the profound effect of the havoc that ensued as a consequence. A resignation by Miller, the former deputy commissioner of public information for the NYPD, would have been a more substantial sign of taking accountability for past significant errors.

EPILOGUE

Who Will Tell Jane Doe's Story?

In McAlary's zeal to get an exclusive, it's likely he paid little mind to how sensationalizing the information he received, which ultimately proved to be incorrect, would affect the life of the victim he was writing about when his first column ran. The desire to "get the scoop" can lead even seasoned journalists to prioritize speed over accuracy and ethical considerations. This rush to publish, often driven by the competitive nature of journalism, had severe consequences.

In Jane Doe's case, this haste to be the first to break a story was particularly devastating, as it involved the publication of unverified information that publicly doubted her account as a sexual assault survivor. The impact of such public doubt of her stranger rape was traumatic for Jane Doe, who had never sought such attention nor anticipated such scrutiny. McAlary's decision to double down on his initial reporting, by promoting and pushing a narrative that continued to cast doubt on Jane Doe's account even as questions about its accuracy arose, compounded the harm done to Jane Doe, extending its reach and impact. His series of columns likely colored broader public perception of her credibility and may have affected the outcome of the official investigation.

In police work, there's been more visibility in recent years around a victim-centered model of investigations, which prioritizes the needs of the victim. This approach represents a significant shift from traditional law enforcement methods that often focused primarily on gathering evidence and apprehending suspects, sometimes at the expense of the victim's well-being. The victim-centered model recognizes that addressing the victim's needs is not only ethically important but can also lead to more effective investigations and better outcomes for all parties involved.

A trauma-informed approach to investigative work avoids re-traumatizing the victim in the process of solving his or her case and understands the neurobiological impacts of trauma and how it affects memory, behavior, and a person's ability to recount their experiences. Law enforcement works with the victim, restoring the sense of security that was lost, by providing comprehensive support which may include connecting victims with mental health services, providing information about their rights and available resources, and offering guidance through the often complex legal system. By incorporating this knowledge into investigative practices, law enforcement can conduct more effective interviews, gather more accurate information, and create an environment where victims feel safe and supported throughout the process.

There is an equivalency in journalism called trauma-informed journalism which adopts a victim-centered approach when reporting on traumatic events like rape, that accounts for the dignity of the victim in the process of reporting the truth. While trauma-informed journalism was not widely practiced or recognized in the mid-1990s when the media landscape in which McAlary was writing his columns was quite different from what would be culturally relevant today, this approach to reporting recognizes that the way a story is reported can have profound effects on the individuals being written about.

A tabloid columnist like Mike McAlary, who at the height of his career was one of the most well-compensated reporters in New York, likely cut his teeth in a newsroom culture where he learned to tailor his writing style to appeal to the broadest audience. In the early days of his journalism career when he was writing for sports for the *New York Daily News* he may have added entertainment value to his content, for greater impact in reaching his readership.

Though tabloid editors are expected to hold columnists to basic journalistic standards, ensuring a balanced and fair representation of facts, it is understandable why, in the world of tabloids, breaking a story trumps rigorous fact-checking when meeting their bottom line. In the cultural mores and social norms of the time, there was no language to discuss what it would mean for a columnist to adhere to a victim-centered approach in a story about rape. Dialogue on compassionate methodology simply didn't exist, and without words to give shape to structure and form, there was also no conceivable return on investment.

Jane Doe was the victim of a stranger rape, sexually violated by a person she did not know, after which she was disbelieved, ridiculed publicly, and gaslighted by a journalist whom she never met, in the time before her case went unsolved and remained cold for two-plus decades. By all accounts, from her perspective, she had been victimized several times over.

Acknowledging how implicit bias over Jane Doe's race and sexual orientation, as a Black lesbian, greatly affected how this case was handled, Commissioner James P. O'Neill, in his October 2018[1] apology to Jane, addressed the department's shortcomings when her case was first investigated: "This rape survivor was suspected of inventing the crime to publicize a planned rally protesting violence against lesbians. I firmly believe that no one in the NYPD would draw such an implausible and ridiculous conclusion today." The acknowledgment of such biases is a significant step toward addressing systemic issues within the police department by improving its relationship with marginalized communities.

He went on to write, "This police department has come a long way since 1994 in our response to sexual assaults and in our understanding of, and respect for, the LGBTQIA+ community. And our Special Victims Squad investigators who pursue instances of sexual assault today have more tools, better training and resources, and greater skills than ever before."

The commissioner's apology and acknowledgment of past failures represent a significant shift in the NYPD's approach to developing more equitable and effective policing practices when handling sensitive cases. By explicitly addressing Jane Doe's sexual orientation, as it related to her rape case, O'Neill demonstrates how implicit bias could result in severe injustices.

Furthermore, O'Neill's statement about the department's progress in understanding and respecting the LGBTQIA+ community also reflects a broader societal shift toward greater acceptance and awareness of diverse sexual orientations and gender identities. This progress is vital for law enforcement agencies, as it can help reduce discrimination and improve allyship with LGBTQIA+ individuals, who have historically faced significant challenges in their interactions with police.

The difference between a good investigator and a great one is the ability and doggedness to remain unbiased, to follow the facts, and to exercise due diligence to avoid harm. This distinction underscores the importance of maintaining objectivity throughout an investigation, regardless of personal beliefs or preconceptions. A great investigator must be able to set aside any potential biases and approach each case with an open mind, allowing the evidence to guide their conclusions rather than fitting evidence to preconceived notions. This is especially cogent in cases where societal prejudices might unwittingly bias the investigative process.

Great investigators must constantly challenge their own assumptions and be willing to reevaluate their perspectives based on new information or evidence. When collecting and analyzing available evidence, great investigators understand the importance of corroborating information from multiple sources and are willing to pursue leads that might challenge their initial hypotheses.

Exercising due diligence to avoid harm is a critical aspect of ethical investigation. Additional requisite training in cultural competence would enable detectives and officers to be effectively responsive and respectful in meeting the needs of victims who have varying needs from diverse backgrounds and populations. Cultural competency training includes developing an awareness of cultural norms, values, and communication styles that may differ from their own, as well as recognizing how cultural factors might influence a victim's response to trauma or their willingness to engage with law enforcement. Training could help investigators avoid misunderstandings or misinterpretations that could potentially derail an investigation by providing tools for more effective communication in the investigative process. This, in turn, can result in more effective investigations, as community members may be more willing to come forward with information or report crimes when they feel understood and respected by law enforcement.

In her statement to *The New York Times*, in the time after her case was solved, Jane Doe lauded Detective Andrea Sorrentino for having worked tirelessly on her case in 1994. Though Sorrentino did not solve the case, her detailed documentation made it possible for me to recreate the case, which led to solving it using the forensic DNA techniques available at the time.

In April of 2013, Attorney Martin Garbus contributed an Op-ed[2] to the *New York Times* after seeing actor Tom Hanks cast in the role of Mike McAlary in Nora Ephron's play *Lucky Guy*, which had its Broadway run at the Broadhurst Theatre. His op-ed served as a powerful reminder of the unresolved injustice surrounding Jane Doe's case and the harm inflicted when McAlary contorted the truth and fabricated facts, forever a stain on his legacy. In his Op-ed, Garbus wrote:

> I believe McAlary damaged her more than the rapist did. . . . I don't doubt McAlary's fortitude, but he did not have the courage to recant his false allegations, much less apologize to the young woman whose life he knowingly damaged at the altar of professional hubris and ambition. . . . It seems most unfortunate that McAlary chose to champion a sodomized man but not a raped woman. And one must reflect on whether one very good deed can undo a very bad one. . . . We all can revisit Mike McAlary's life and death on Broadway thanks to Ephron's play. But who will tell us Jane Doe's story?

This book is my earnest answer to the question posed. Garbus's criticism of McAlary's failure to recant his errors underscored the profound and lasting damage that was inflicted through callous and irresponsible journalism. By retelling Jane Doe's story, and exploring the complex interplay between journalism, justice, and survivorship, this work aims to provide a counternarrative to the one that has dominated public discourse, by offering a more nuanced and empathetic understanding of the events and their lasting impact.

NOTES

CHAPTER 2

1. Levitt, Leonard. "NYPD Spokesman Apologies to Writers." *City Briefs, Newsday* (New York, NY), May 27, 1994. https://www.newspapers.com/newspage/706906514/.

2. Levitt, Leonard. "NYPD Spokesman Apologies to Writers." *City Briefs, Newsday* (New York, NY), May 27, 1994. https://www.newspapers.com/newspage/706906514/.

3. Levitt, Leonard. "NYPD Spokesman Apologies to Writers." *City Briefs, Newsday* (New York, NY), May 27, 1994. https://www.newspapers.com/newspage/706906514/.

4. Anti-Violence Project. Accessed September 27, 2024. https://avp.org/.

5. Krauss, Clifford. "Bratton Says Police Were Wrong to Air Doubt in Rape Case." *New York Times*, April 30, 1994. https://www.nytimes.com/1994/04/30/nyregion/bratton-says-police-were-wrong-to-air-doubt-in-rape-case.html.

6. Krauss, Clifford. "Bratton Says Police Were Wrong to Air Doubt in Rape Case." *New York Times*, April 30, 1994. https://www.nytimes.com/1994/04/30/nyregion/bratton-says-police-were-wrong-to-air-doubt-in-rape-case.html.

7. Krauss, Clifford. "Bratton Says Police Were Wrong to Air Doubt in Rape Case." *New York Times*, April 30, 1994. https://www.nytimes.com/1994/04/30/nyregion/bratton-says-police-were-wrong-to-air-doubt-in-rape-case.html.

8. "Ire Over Rape Case, Groups Blast Skeptical Police." *New York Daily News*, April 29, 1994, 20. https://www.newspapers.com/image/472810771.

9. "Murder of Carol Stuart." *Wikipedia*. Last modified September 23, 2024. https://en.wikipedia.org/wiki/Murder_of_Carol_Stuart.

10. *Retro Report*. The New York Times. YouTube video, 13:49. Posted by Retro Report, May 20, 2013. https://www.youtube.com/watch?v=T78DwdFUq0c.

11. Winerip, Michael. "Revisiting the Tawana Brawley Rape Scandal." *New York Times*, June 3, 2013. https://www.nytimes.com/2013/06/03/booming/revisiting-the-tawana-brawley-rape-scandal.html.

CHAPTER 3

1. Rashbaum, William K., and Wendell Jamieson. "Another Prospect Park Rape." *Newsday* (New York, NY), April 27, 1994, 1. https://www.newspapers.com/image/706861307.

2. Vance, Cyrus R., Jr. *Test Every Kit: Results from the Manhattan District Attorney's Office's Sexual Assault Kit Backlog Elimination Grant Program*. New York: Manhattan District Attorney's Office, March 2019. https://www.manhattanda.org/wp-content/uploads/2019/03/Test-Every-Kit-Results-from-the-Manhattan-District-Attorneys-Offices-Sexual-Assault-Kit-Backlog-Eliminaton-Grant-Program.pdf.

3. *KSDK News*. YouTube video, 3:15. Posted by KSDK News. https://www.youtube.com/watch?v=o5K0d6KNHEU.

4. "About RAINN." *RAINN*. Accessed September 27, 2024. https://www.rainn.org/about-rain.

5. "Victims of Sexual Violence: Statistics." *RAINN*. Accessed September 27, 2024. https://www.rainn.org/statistics/victims-sexual-violence.

6. "Less than 1 Percent of Rapes Lead to Felony Convictions. At Least 89 Percent of Victims Face Emotional and Physical Consequences." *Washington Post*, October 6, 2018. https://www.washingtonpost.com/business/2018/10/06/less-than-percent-rapes-lead-felony-convictions-least-percent-victims-face-emotional-physical-consequences/.

7. Goodman, Emily Jane. "State Removes Statute of Limitations for Rape Cases." *Gotham Gazette*, June 5, 2006. https://www.gothamgazette.com/criminal-justice/1381-state-removes-statute-of-limitations-for-rape-cases.

8. McAlary, Mike. "Rape Hoax the Real Crime." *Daily News* (New York, NY), April 28, 1994, 8. https://www.newspapers.com.

9. McAlary, Mike. "I'm Right But That's No Reason to Cheer." *New York Daily News* (New York, NY), May 13, 1994.

CHAPTER 4

1. Weiss, Murray. "NYPD Lab Found Semen on Park Victim." *New York Post*, April 1994. https://www.newspapers.com.

2. Weiss, Murray. "NYPD Lab Found Semen on Park Victim." *New York Post*, April 1994. https://www.newspapers.com.

3. Garbus, Martin, with Stanley Cohen. *Tough Talk*. New York: Three Rivers Press, 1998.

4. Levitt, Leonard. "One Police Plaza Confidential: Park Rape Case: Whose Hoax?" *New York Newsday*, May 23, 1994.

5. Levitt, Leonard. "One Police Plaza Confidential: Park Rape Case: Whose Hoax?" *New York Newsday*, May 23, 1994.

CHAPTER 5

1. Levitt, Leonard. "One Police Plaza Confidential: Park Rape Case: Whose Hoax?" *New York Newsday*, May 23, 1994.

2. Garbus, Martin, with Stanley Cohen. *Tough Talk*. New York: Three Rivers Press, 1998.

3. In *Tough Talk*, Marty Garbus asserts that Rotello's conversation with Miller occurred on May 14, 1995 (Garbus, *Tough Talk*).

4. Rotello, Gabriel. "What I Never Told Nora Ephron About Mike McAlary." *HuffPost*, April 3, 2013. https://www.huffpost.com/entry/what-i-never-told-nora-ephron-about-mike-mcalary_b_3000722.

5. Rotello, Gabriel. "What I Never Told Nora Ephron About Mike McAlary." *HuffPost*, April 3, 2013. https://www.huffpost.com/entry/what-i-never-told-nora-ephron-about-mike-mcalary_b_3000722.

6. Krauss, Clifford. "Bratton Says Police Were Wrong to Air Doubt in Rape Case." *New York Times*, April 30, 1994. https://www.nytimes.com/1994

/04/30/nyregion/bratton-says-police-were-wrong-to-air-doubt-in-rape-case.html.

7. Rotello, Gabriel. "What I Never Told Nora Ephron About Mike McAlary." *HuffPost*, April 3, 2013. https://www.huffpost.com/entry/what-i-never-told-nora-ephron-about-mike-mcalary_b_3000722.

8. Straw, Joseph, and Larry McShane. "Bratton: CBS News Correspondent John Miller to Be NYPD's Counter-terrorism Chief." *NY Daily News*, January 10, 2019. https://www.nydailynews.com/new-york/bratton-taps-cbs-john-miller-counter-terror-post-article-1.1564576.

9. *CBS New York*. "John Miller's Retirement." YouTube video, Posted by CBS New York. https://www.youtube.com/watch?v=Rmv_-UAOtc8.

10. "Lucky Guy (Play)." *Wikipedia*. Last modified September 27, 2024. https://en.wikipedia.org/wiki/Lucky_Guy_(play).

11. Conley, Kirstan, Larry Celona, and Shawn Cohen. "Cops Solve 1994 Prospect Park Rape Case with New DNA Testing Technology." *News.com.au*. Accessed September 27, 2024. https://www.news.com.au/lifestyle/real-life/news-life/cops-solve-1994-prospect-park-rape-case-with-new-dna-testing-technology/news-story/4a108e725e27e8ad5add7d828117ea1a.

12. Garbus, Martin, with Stanley Cohen. *Tough Talk*. New York: Three Rivers Press, 1998, pg. 246.

13. Garbus, Martin, with Stanley Cohen. *Tough Talk*. New York: Three Rivers Press, 1998, pg. 242.

14. Garbus, Martin, with Stanley Cohen. *Tough Talk*. New York: Three Rivers Press, 1998, pg. 242.

15. *Jill Abramson, Former Executive Director of The New York Times*. YouTube video, Posted by YouTube, https://www.youtube.com/watch?v=7nVFla_qx1I.

16. Garbus, Martin, with Stanley Cohen. *Tough Talk*. New York: Three Rivers Press, 1998, pg. 261.

17. "Mike McAlary's 1997 Pulitzer Prize-Winning Abner Louima Columns." *NY Daily News*, August 13, 2007, updated January 12, 2019. https://www.nydailynews.com/2007/08/13/mike-mcalarys-1997-pulitzer-prize-winning-abner-louima-columns/.

CHAPTER 6

1. Garbus, Martin, with Stanley Cohen. *Tough Talk*. New York: Three Rivers Press, 1998, pg. 241.

2. Garbus, Martin, with Stanley Cohen. *Tough Talk*. New York: Three Rivers Press, 1998, pg. 242.

3. Garbus, Martin, with Stanley Cohen. *Tough Talk*. New York: Three Rivers Press, 1998, pg. 247.

4. McKinley, James C., Jr. "Judge Decides Rape Victim in Lawsuit Is Public Figure." *New York Times*, July 21, 1995. https://www.nytimes.com/1995/07/21/nyregion/judge-decides-rape-victim-in-lawsuit-is-public-figure.html.

5. Van Natta, Don, Jr. "Facts, Lies and Opinions on Trial." *New York Times*, January 29, 1996. https://www.nytimes.com/1996/01/29/nyregion/facts-lies-and-opinions-on-trial.html.

6. Garbus, Martin, with Stanley Cohen. *Tough Talk*. New York: Three Rivers Press, 1998, pg. 253.

7. Garbus, Martin, with Stanley Cohen. *Tough Talk*. New York: Three Rivers Press, 1998, pg. 254.

8. Garbus, Martin, with Stanley Cohen. *Tough Talk*. New York: Three Rivers Press, 1998, pg. 262.

9. Sullivan, John. "Columnist Wins a Suit on Articles about Rape." *New York Times*, February 7, 1997.
https://www.nytimes.com/1997/02/07/nyregion/columnist-wins-a-suit-on-articles-about-rape.html?searchResultPosition=1.

10. Parascandola, Rocco, and Thomas Tracy. "DNA Evidence Points to Career Rapist in 1994 Prospect Park Rape." *NY Daily News*, January 9, 2018. https://www.nydailynews.com/2018/01/09/dna-evidence-points-to-career-rapist-in-1994-prospect-park-rape/.

CHAPTER 7

1. New York State Division of Criminal Justice Services. "New York State DNA Databank." Accessed September 27, 2024. https://www.criminaljustice.ny.gov/forensic/dnadatabank.htm.

2. Goodman, Emily Jane. "State Removes Statute of Limitations for Rape Cases." *Gotham Gazette*, June 5, 2006. https://www.gothamgazette.com/criminal-justice/1381-state-removes-statute-of-limitations-for-rape-cases.

3. New York State Assembly. "Press Release: Assembly Passes Bill to Remove Statute of Limitations for Rape Cases." May 10, 2006. https://assembly.state.ny.us/Press/20060510/.

4. Preston, Julia. "In New York, Power of DNA Spurs Call to Abolish Statute of Limitations for Rape." *New York Times*, January 2, 2006. https://

www.nytimes.com/2006/01/02/nyregion/in-new-york-power-of-dna-spurs-call-to-abolish-statute-of.html.

5. Ravitz, Jessica. "The Story Behind the First Rape Kit." *CNN*, November 21, 2015. https://www.cnn.com/2015/11/20/health/rape-kit-history/index.html.

6. National Forensic Science Technology Center. "Advancing Justice Through DNA Technology: Principles of Forensic DNA for Officers of the Court." Accessed September 27, 2024. https://projects.nfstc.org/otc/module4/4.1.010.htm.

CHAPTER 8

1. "Metro News Brief." *New York Times*, October 30, 1997.

2. Investigative timeline, created by, S.A. Mathers and Michael Osgood, 2017.
   08/17/1995: 088 Precinct; Rape 1, Sodomy 1, Robbery
   11/14/1995: 088 Precinct Rape 1, Sodomy 1
   11/16/1995: 088 Precinct: Robbery (female victim was sixteen years old)

3. Bilkis, Stephen. "James Webb Was Paroled from the Orleans Correctional Facility." *New York Criminal Lawyer 24/7 Blog*, December 15, 2011. https://www.newyorkcriminallawyer24-7blog.com/james_webb_was_paroled_from_th/.

4. Bilkis, Stephen. "James Webb Was Paroled from the Orleans Correctional Facility." *New York Criminal Lawyer 24/7 Blog*, December 15, 2011. https://www.newyorkcriminallawyer24-7blog.com/james_webb_was_paroled_from_th/.

5. Kings County Supreme Court. Brooklyn, NY. Part of the Second Judicial District of New York State.

6. *Webb v. Goldstein*, U.S. District Court, Eastern District of New York, No. 00-885672624, September 29, 2000. https://case-law.vlex.com/vid/webb-v-goldstein-no-885672624.

CHAPTER 9

1. Conley, Kirstan, Larry Celona, and Shawn Cohen. "Cops Crack Infamous Prospect Park Rape Case with DNA." *New York Post*, January 9, 2018. https://nypost.com/2018/01/09/cops-crack-infamous-prospect-park-rape-case-with-dna/.

2. Conley, Kirstan, Larry Celona, and Shawn Cohen. "Cops Crack Infamous Prospect Park Rape Case with DNA." *New York Post*, January 9, 2018. https://nypost.com/2018/01/09/cops-crack-infamous-prospect-park-rape-case-with-dna/.

3. Parascandola, Rocco, and Thomas Tracy. "DNA Evidence Points to Career Rapist in 1994 Prospect Park Rape." *NY Daily News*, January 9, 2018. https://www.nydailynews.com/2018/01/09/dna-evidence-points-to-career-rapist-in-1994-prospect-park-rape/.

4. "A Request for an Apology: Statement from Victim in a 1994 Brooklyn Rape Case." *New York Times*, January 12, 2018. https://www.nytimes.com/2018/01/12/nyregion/statement-from-victim-in-a-1994-brooklyn-rape-case.html.

5. Garbus, Martin, with Stanley Cohen. *Tough Talk*. New York: Three Rivers Press, 1998, pg. 254.

6. Baker, Al. "For Brooklyn Rape Victim, a Long-Awaited Apology from Police." *New York Times*, January 12, 2018. https://www.nytimes.com/2018/01/12/nyregion/for-brooklyn-rape-victim-a-long-awaited-apology-from-police.html.

7. "A Request for an Apology: Statement from Victim in a 1994 Brooklyn Rape Case." *New York Times*, January 12, 2018. https://www.nytimes.com/2018/01/12/nyregion/statement-from-victim-in-a-1994-brooklyn-rape-case.html.

8. New York City Police Department. "Police Commissioner James P. O'Neill's Apology to the Survivor of the 1994 Prospect Park Rape Case." October 28, 2018. https://www.nyc.gov/site/nypd/news/s1028/police-commissioner-james-p-o-neill-s-apology-the-survivor-the-1994-prospect-park-rape-case.

9. Southall, Ashley. "24 Years Later, Woman Who Was Maligned After Rape Gets Apology from Police Commissioner." *New York Times*, October 28, 2018. https://www.nytimes.com/2018/10/28/nyregion/apology-police-prospect-park-rape.html.

10. Annese, John. "In Rare Public Apology, NYPD Commissioner Tells 1994 Rape Victim He Is 'Profoundly Sorry'." *Governing*, October 29, 2018. https://www.governing.com/archive/tns-prospect-park-rape-nypd-commissioner-apology.html.

11. Garbus, Martin, with Stanley Cohen. *Tough Talk*. New York: Three Rivers Press, 1998, pgs. 256–257.

EPILOGUE

1. New York City Police Department. "Police Commissioner James P. O'Neill's Apology to the Survivor of the 1994 Prospect Park Rape Case." October 28, 2018.

2. Garbus, Martin. "The Damage Done by a 'Lucky Guy'." *New York Times*, April 2, 2013. https://www.nytimes.com/2013/04/03/opinion/the-damage-done-by-a-lucky-guy.html.

BIBLIOGRAPHY

"A Request for an Apology: Statement From Victim in a 1994 Brooklyn Rape Case." *New York Times*, January 12, 2018. https://www.nytimes.com/2018/01/12/nyregion/statement-from-victim-in-a-1994-brooklyn-rape-case.html.

"About RAINN." *RAINN*. Accessed September 27, 2024. https://www.rainn.org/about-rai.

Annese, John. "In Rare Public Apology, NYPD Commissioner Tells 1994 Rape Victim He Is 'Profoundly Sorry'." *Governing*, October 29, 2018. https://www.governing.com/archive/tns-prospect-park-rape-nypd-commissioner-apology.html.

Anti-Violence Project. Accessed September 27, 2024. https://avp.org/.

Baker, Al. "For Brooklyn Rape Victim, a Long-Awaited Apology From Police." *New York Times*, January 12, 2018. https://www.nytimes.com/2018/01/12/nyregion/for-brooklyn-rape-victim-a-long-awaited-apology-from-police.html.

Bilkis, Stephen. "James Webb Was Paroled from the Orleans Correctional Facility." *New York Criminal Lawyer 24/7 Blog*, December 15, 2011. https://www.newyorkcriminallawyer24-7blog.com/james_webb_was_paroled_from_th/.

CBS New York. "John Miller's Retirement." YouTube video, [video length]. Posted by CBS New York, [date of publication]. https://www.youtube.com/watch?v=Rmv_-UAOtc8.

Conley, Kirstan, Larry Celona, and Shawn Cohen. "Cops Crack Infamous Prospect Park Rape Case with DNA." *New York Post*, January 9, 2018. https://nypost.com/2018/01/09/cops-crack-infamous-prospect-park-rape-case-with-dna/.

Conley, Kirstan, Larry Celona, and Shawn Cohen. "Cops Solve 1994 Prospect Park Rape Case with New DNA Testing Technology." *News.com.au*. Accessed September 27, 2024. https://www.news.com.au/lifestyle/real-life/news-life/cops-solve-1994-prospect-park-rape-case-with-new-dna-testing-technology/news-story/4a108e725e27e8ad5add7d828117ea1a.

Garbus, Martin. "The Damage Done by a 'Lucky Guy'." *New York Times*, April 2, 2013. https://www.nytimes.com/2013/04/03/opinion/the-damage-done-by-a-lucky-guy.html.

Garbus, Martin, with Stanley Cohen. *Tough Talk*. New York: Three Rivers Press, 1998.

Goodman, Emily Jane. "State Removes Statute of Limitations for Rape Cases." *Gotham Gazette*, June 5, 2006. https://www.gothamgazette.com/criminal-justice/1381-state-removes-statute-of-limitations-for-rape-cases.

"In *Tough Talk*," Marty Garbus asserts that Rotello's conversation with Miller occurred on May 14, 1995 (Garbus, *Tough Talk*).

"Ire Over Rape Case, Groups Blast Skeptical Police." *New York Daily News*, April 29, 1994, 20. https://www.newspapers.com/image/472810771.

Jill Abramson, Former Executive Director of The New York Times. YouTube video, [video length]. Posted by YouTube. https://www.youtube.com/watch?v=7nVFla_qx1I.

Kings County Supreme Court. Brooklyn, NY. Part of the Second Judicial District of New York State.

Krauss, Clifford. "Bratton Says Police Were Wrong to Air Doubt in Rape Case." *New York Times*, April 30, 1994. https://www.nytimes.com/1994/04/30/nyregion/bratton-says-police-were-wrong-to-air-doubt-in-rape-case.html.

KSDK News. YouTube video, 3:15. Posted by KSDK News. https://www.youtube.com/watch?v=o5K0d6KNHEU.

"Less than 1 Percent of Rapes Lead to Felony Convictions. At Least 89 Percent of Victims Face Emotional and Physical Consequences." *Washington Post*, October 6, 2018. https://www.washingtonpost.com/business/2018/10/06/less-than-percent-rapes-lead-felony-convictions-least-percent-victims-face-emotional-physical-consequences/.

Levitt, Leonard. "NYPD Spokesman Apologies to Writers." *City Briefs, Newsday* (New York, NY), May 27, 1994. https://www.newspapers.com/newspage/706906514/.

Levitt, Leonard. "One Police Plaza Confidential: Park Rape Case: Whose Hoax?" *New York Newsday*, May 23, 1994.

"Lucky Guy (Play)." *Wikipedia.* Last modified September 27, 2024. https://en.wikipedia.org/wiki/Lucky_Guy_(play).

Mathers, Sarah and Michael Osgood. "Investigative Timeline." Prepared October 2017–January 2018

McAlary, Mike. "I'm Right But That's No Reason to Cheer." *New York Daily News* (New York, NY), May 13, 1994.

McAlary, Mike. "Rape Hoax the Real Crime." *Daily News* (New York, NY), April 28, 1994, 8. https://www.newspapers.com.

McKinley, James C., Jr. "Judge Decides Rape Victim In Lawsuit Is Public Figure." *New York Times*, July 21, 1995. https://www.nytimes.com/1995/07/21/nyregion/judge-decides-rape-victim-in-lawsuit-is-public-figure.html.

"Metro News Brief." *New York Times*, October 30, 1997.

"Mike McAlary's 1997 Pulitzer Prize-Winning Abner Louima Columns." *NY Daily News*, August 13, 2007, updated January 12, 2019. https://www.nydailynews.com/2007/08/13/mike-mcalarys-1997-pulitzer-prize-winning-abner-louima-columns/.

"Murder of Carol Stuart." *Wikipedia.* Last modified September 23, 2024. https://en.wikipedia.org/wiki/Murder_of_Carol_Stuart.

National Forensic Science Technology Center. "Advancing Justice Through DNA Technology: Principles of Forensic DNA for Officers of the Court." Accessed September 27, 2024. https://projects.nfstc.org/otc/module4/4.1.010.htm.

New York City Police Department. "Police Commissioner James P. O'Neill's Apology to the Survivor of the 1994 Prospect Park Rape Case." October 28, 2018. https://www.nyc.gov/site/nypd/news/s1028/police-commissioner-james-p-o-neill-s-apology-the-survivor-the-1994-prospect-park-rape-case.

New York State Assembly. "Press Release: Assembly Passes Bill to Remove Statute of Limitations for Rape Cases." May 10, 2006. https://assembly.state.ny.us/Press/20060510/.

New York State Division of Criminal Justice Services. "New York State DNA Databank." Accessed September 27, 2024. https://www.criminaljustice.ny.gov/forensic/dnadatabank.htm.

Parascandola, Rocco, and Thomas Tracy. "DNA Evidence Points to Career Rapist in 1994 Prospect Park Rape." *NY Daily News*, January 9, 2018. https://www.nydailynews.com/2018/01/09/dna-evidence-points-to-career-rapist-in-1994-prospect-park-rape/.

Preston, Julia. "In New York, Power of DNA Spurs Call to Abolish Statute of Limitations for Rape." *New York Times*, January 2, 2006. https://www.nytimes.com/2006/01/02/nyregion/in-new-york-power-of-dna-spurs-call-to-abolish-statute-of.html.

Rashbaum, William K., and Wendell Jamieson. "Another Prospect Park Rape." *Newsday* (New York, NY), April 27, 1994, 1. https://www.newspapers.com/image/706861307.

Ravitz, Jessica. "The Story Behind the First Rape Kit." *CNN*, November 21, 2015. https://www.cnn.com/2015/11/20/health/rape-kit-history/index.html.

Retro Report. The New York Times. YouTube video, 13:49. Posted by Retro Report, May 20, 2013. https://www.youtube.com/watch?v=T78DwdFUq0c.

Rotello, Gabriel. "What I Never Told Nora Ephron About Mike McAlary." *HuffPost*, April 3, 2013. https://www.huffpost.com/entry/what-i-never-told-nora-ephron-about-mike-mcalary_b_3000722.

Southall, Ashley. "24 Years Later, Woman Who Was Maligned After Rape Gets Apology From Police Commissioner." *New York Times*, October 28, 2018. https://www.nytimes.com/2018/10/28/nyregion/apology-police-prospect-park-rape.html.

Straw, Joseph, and Larry McShane. "Bratton: CBS News Correspondent John Miller to Be NYPD's Counter-terrorism Chief." *NY Daily News*, January 10, 2019. https://www.nydailynews.com/new-york/bratton-taps-cbs-john-miller-counter-terror-post-article-1.1564576.

Sullivan, John. "Columnist Wins a Suit on Articles about Rape." *New York Times*, February 7, 1997. https://www.nytimes.com/1997/02/07/nyregion/columnist-wins-a-suit-on-articles-about-rape.html?searchResultPosition=1.

Van Natta, Don, Jr. "Facts, Lies and Opinions on Trial." *New York Times*, January 29, 1996. https://www.nytimes.com/1996/01/29/nyregion/facts-lies-and-opinions-on-trial.html.

Vance, Cyrus R., Jr. *Test Every Kit: Results from the Manhattan District Attorney's Office's Sexual Assault Kit Backlog Elimination Grant Program.* New York: Manhattan District Attorney's Office, March 2019. https://www.manhattanda.org/wp-content/uploads/2019/03/Test-Every-Kit-Results-from-the-Manhattan-District-Attorneys-Offices-Sexual-Assault-Kit-Backlog-Eliminaton-Grant-Program.pdf.

"Victims of Sexual Violence: Statistics." *RAINN*. Accessed September 27, 2024. https://www.rainn.org/statistics/victims-sexual-violence.

Webb v. Goldstein, U.S. District Court, Eastern District of New York, No. 00-885672624, September 29, 2000. https://case-law.vlex.com/vid/webb-v-goldstein-no-885672624.

Weiss, Murray. "NYPD Lab Found Semen on Park Victim." *New York Post*, April 1994. https://www.newspapers.com.

Winerip, Michael. "Revisiting the Tawana Brawley Rape Scandal." *New York Times*, June 3, 2013. https://www.nytimes.com/2013/06/03/booming/revisiting-the-tawana-brawley-rape-scandal.html.

INDEX

ABOUT THE AUTHOR

Sarah A. Mathers is a retired First Grade Detective with the New York City Police Department, where she dedicated over twenty years to investigating complex cases, including those involving sexual assault. With a background in communications and a master's degree in criminal justice, as well as experience as an adjunct professor, Mathers brings a unique blend of skills to her storytelling. Her commitment to justice and deep understanding of human behavior inform her compelling narratives. Through her work, she aims to shed light on the realities of law enforcement and survivors' stories that often go untold.